Doll Crafts

A Kid's Guide to Making Simple Dolls, Clothing, Accessories, and Houses

Laurie Carlson

CHICAGO
REVIEW
PRESS

Copyright © 2018 by Laurie Carlson
All rights reserved
Published by Chicago Review Press Incorporated
814 North Franklin Street
Chicago, Illinois 60610
ISBN 978-1-61373-778-1

Library of Congress Cataloging-in-Publication Data
Names: Carlson, Laurie M., 1952– author.
Title: Doll crafts : a kid's guide to making simple dolls, clothing,
    accessories, and houses / Laurie Carlson.
Description: Chicago, Illinois : Chicago Review Press Incorporated, [2018] |
    Audience: Age 7+.
Identifiers: LCCN 2017013441 (print) | LCCN 2017025868 (ebook) | ISBN
    9781613737798 (adobe pdf) | ISBN 9781613737811 (epub) | ISBN 9781613737804
    (kindle) | ISBN 9781613737781 (trade paper)
Subjects: LCSH: Dollmaking—Juvenile literature. | Doll
    clothes—Patterns—Juvenile literature. | Dollhouses—Juvenile literature.
Classification: LCC TT175 (ebook) | LCC TT175 .C315 2017 (print) | DDC
    745.592/21—dc23
LC record available at https://lccn.loc.gov/2017013441

Cover and interior design: Sarah Olson
Cover illustrations: Jim Spence
Interior illustrations: Lindsey Cleworth Schauer

Printed in the United States of America
5 4 3 2 1

Contents

Introduction

Dolls have always been a part of people's lives. Before they were mass produced in factories, every doll was made by hand, and every doll was unique. Most dolls were created especially for a certain person.

Childhood dolls are special, and even when you are older, you will probably remember your special doll. That's because dolls—especially if they were handmade—are unique among toys and possessions. They can be like friends to us, and it's fun to imagine other worlds while playing with dolls. The feeling that you get sharing the world with a doll can be hard to explain to others; it just makes you feel good. Dolls may be simple, delightful, or mysterious. Like you and me, every handmade doll is unique.

As you begin to make dolls, you'll join the ranks of other doll makers over the centuries who have used skill and imagination and whatever materials were available to make their dolls. Welcome to the group! Make a few simple dolls to get started, and then develop skills and use personal touches to create one-of-a-kind pieces of art. Give dolls as gifts to people you like, and teach friends how to make them, too. You can never have too many dolls! If you do get carried away, start your own doll collection or even a doll museum, where you can share your interest with everyone.

A Note on Terms

You'll see that sometimes the directions refer to the "good," "wrong," or "right" side of your material or fabric. That doesn't mean one side is better or worse, and it doesn't refer to the right side as opposed to

the left side. Those terms just refer to the side of the fabric that you eventually want showing (the "good" or "right" side) and the side that won't be showing (the "wrong" side) on your finished doll.

Happy doll crafting!

Dolls Are Not Just Toys

Dolls represent humans, and through much of history they were not toys but served important purposes. Dolls were made as good luck charms or talismans. In northern Europe, a "kitchen witch" doll was thought to bring good luck to the house. In ancient Japan, dolls were kept on fishing ships so that if a dangerous storm threatened, fishermen could throw the doll overboard, hoping to ensure the safety of human lives on the boat. Native Americans and Europeans made small dolls they buried in the soil to ensure good crops. Healers believed dolls could take pain and disease from someone's body into the doll, as a cure.

WELCOME TO THE WORKSHOP!
Doll Maker's Toolbox

Tools

Every doll maker needs a collection of tools and materials. You don't have to buy a lot of stuff, though. Start with what you have at home. Find a small old suitcase, lunch box, or cardboard box with a lid. Fill it with tools and small supplies, including:

- Hand-sewing needles and pins
- Pincushion
- Scissors
- Sewing thread: black, white, and flesh tones. Start with these basic colors, and add more colors to match projects.
- Embroidery thread in a variety of colors
- Fine-tip permanent markers: black, brown, orange, and pink
- Design book: any type of notebook or sketchbook
- Colored pencils for creating designs and patterns
- Buttons, beads, and other trimmings: your toolbox is a great place to store all those loose items so you know where to find them when you need them.

Materials

Devote a second box to doll materials. Materials will vary from project to project, but you'll need to start gathering a variety so you have plenty of options when you're ready to begin making dolls. For doll clothing, choose lightweight fabrics with small-scale prints to match the doll's size. Avoid fabrics that unravel easily, or the clothing will look messy and could fall apart. Below are some ideas for starting your collection of materials.

- Felt pieces in several colors
- A selection of fasteners, such as small buttons, sew-on snaps, tiny buckles, and pieces of Velcro fastener tape
- Socks in a variety of colors and sizes. These will be handy for making sock dolls as well as clothing for other dolls. Sport socks, wool socks, and nylon stockings will all be useful.
- Discarded clothing, curtains, towels, and other fabric scraps. Any fabrics that can be saved and repurposed belong in your doll maker's treasure trove.
- Other odds and ends: empty thread spools, flexible wire, wooden spoons, colorful paper, ribbons, discarded jewelry, and almost anything else. Whatever you gather can be used eventually.

Doll crafting is easier when you have a variety of materials to work with, but don't worry if you don't have the "right" materials. Artists use whatever is

Doll Materials—What's Next?

Cloth dolls have always been popular, and they can be made at home by hand. Over the centuries, dolls have also been made from wood, clay, leather, or wax. But the search for a hard material that doesn't break and doesn't cost much to make has led doll makers to try a variety of other materials, too. As technology changed, dolls were made of whatever new material was on the market. About 300 years ago, an unbreakable mixture called composition was created by mixing sawdust, plaster, and glue. Doll makers also used papier-mâché, made by pressing paper or wood pulp into molds, then dipping the painted and finished doll in wax to make it look realistic. After World War II, plastics that didn't crack or shrink became popular. Since then, most store-bought dolls have been made from plastics. The next step may be using 3-D printers to create your own plastic dolls. After that, who knows what material will be invented?

available in a creative way. Being creative means finding ways to use what you have on hand. Remember, you must experiment. Don't worry that you are wasting or ruining materials. That's all part of gaining experience and experimenting.

All About Eyes

Dolls' eyes are important because they are what bring dolls to life. There are many different materials and types of eyes; the doll's personality and style will help determine which to use. Whatever style of eyes you choose, be sure the mouth, nose, and brows are done with the same technique.

Eyes can be made in several ways. You can paint them with acrylic paints using a tiny pointed brush. You can draw them with fine-tip permanent markers. You can cut pieces from felt and sew or glue them to the doll. You can embroider eyes very easily—and they will never come off. Or you can purchase glue-on eyes or plastic "safety eyes" that snap together. Buttons also work, whether they are flat or have a shank.

Safety first: If a child younger than three years old will be handling the doll, do not use small parts that can fall off and get into the child's mouth. Children can choke on buttons, snaps, beads, or buckles. Do not give them tiny dolls that can fit into their

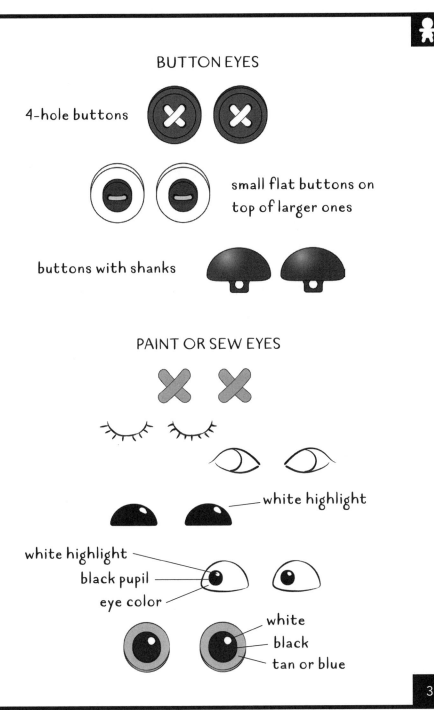

BUTTON EYES

4-hole buttons

small flat buttons on top of larger ones

buttons with shanks

PAINT OR SEW EYES

white highlight

white highlight
black pupil
eye color

white
black
tan or blue

mouths. If you are making a doll for someone between the ages of three and six years old, it's still a good idea to use "safety eyes" rather than buttons or glue-on plastic eyes.

Make a Face "Idea Bank"

Set aside some pages in your design notebook to sketch ideas for different kinds of faces. Gather ideas from cartoons, advertisements, or your own imagination. Draw eyes, noses, mouths, and facial expressions. The direction the eyes are looking—or even closed lids—can make a big difference in a doll's attitude. So can eyebrows—arched, hairy, tiny, and so on. Sketch out lots of expressive ideas so when you are ready to make a doll's face you can pick features that fit the doll's personality.

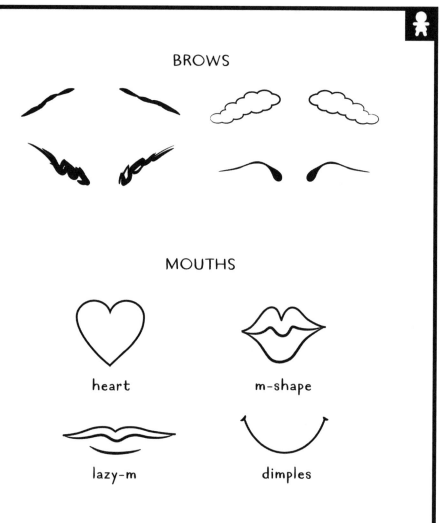

BROWS

MOUTHS

heart

m-shape

lazy-m

dimples

EXPRESSIONS

surprised   relaxed

LOCATING EYES

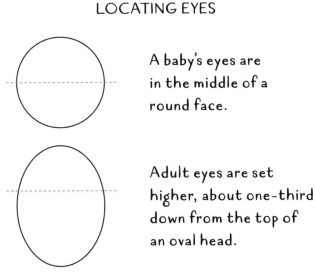

A baby's eyes are in the middle of a round face.

Adult eyes are set higher, about one-third down from the top of an oval head.

LOCATING EARS

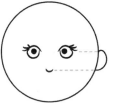

Ears sit between the center of the eye and the bottom of the nose.

Hairy Ideas

Dolls' hair is as fun to work with as people's hair. It can be cut and styled any way you want and can be made in any color. People's hair comes in all sorts of colors and textures, so of course a doll's can, too. A doll's hair is part of its personality, so go all out—wild colors, textures, and lengths—or try something more traditional. Be natural or be fantastic—it's up to you, the artist. The material you choose for hair should fit the doll. Perhaps it needs a soft bit of fluff stuck right on top of the head, or maybe it would look better with thick yarn braids. Doll hair can be made from yarn, craft fur, human hair pieces from beauty supply stores, and more. Some dolls just need a bit of paint for hair—or even just a hat on a bald head.

Yarn is a favorite material for doll hair, but try out other things, too. Cut up old sweaters into strips and sew them onto the doll's head. Old cashmere sweaters are great for this. Wash and dry them at high temperatures, which will shrink the cashmere and create a felt. Felt from the fabric store can be cut to the doll's head shape and stitched to make a cap-like wig, or cut it into longer strips and sew it to the head. If you want kinky, curly hair, unravel an old sweater and reuse the yarn.

Craft Fur Wig

Craft fur is made of synthetic fiber and can be brushed with a hairbrush. It makes soft, thick wigs but doesn't work well for long hairstyles as the hair fibers just aren't very long. You can purchase it in a variety of colors at most fabric or craft supply stores.

MATERIALS

Measuring tape
Craft fur
Pen or fine-tip marker
Scissors with pointed tips
Needle and thread to match craft
    fur
Sewing pins
Extra stuffing (optional)
Hairbrush

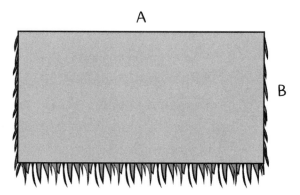

● Measure across the doll's head along the front scalp line, going from ear to ear. That number is A. Measure from one ear (or where an ear would be) to the center back of the head. That number is B. Working on the "wrong" (nonhairy) side of the craft fur, with the hairs running up and down like the drawing, measure a rectangle to match your A and B measurements. It should be A across, as that part will lie across the head from ear to ear. B will be the shorter side. Use a pen or marker to draw the rectangle shape on the back of the craft fur. Cut it out with scissors, working from the back, so you don't cut through all the hairs. Use the tips of the scissors to snip through the backing that holds the hairs, being careful not to cut the furry hair as you go.

Fold the rectangle in half, with the furry side inside. Stitch the edges together in a seam that curves a bit along the corner. Trim away the extra bulk in the corner so it won't create a bump under the wig.

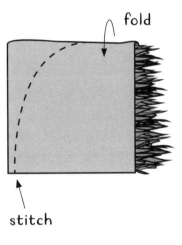

fold

stitch

Turn the wig fur-side out. Pin in place on the doll's head and stitch the wig to the head, sewing along the wig edge and into the doll's head fabric. You may need to tuck stuffing under the wig to fill out the shape before stitching it in place.

When finished, brush the wig with a hairbrush and trim the ends around the face if they need it.

Yarn Hair

This is the easiest way to make yarn hair. It works best for small dolls or short-haired dolls. You'll use only one color of yarn for this method.

MATERIALS

Yarn
Measuring tape
Scissors
Needle and thread to match yarn
Craft glue (optional)

◉ Cut a piece of yarn about 6 inches long. Set aside. Hold one hand stiff and wrap loops of yarn around it several times.

Slip the loops off carefully and slide one end of the 6-inch piece of yarn through the loops. Tie the loops together and knot securely. Set the bundle of loops aside and make several more bundles. Slip scissors through the loops and cut through the ends of the loops.

Stitch or glue the yarn bundles to the doll's head. Put a dot of glue on the center of the loop and position it on the head. Make more bundles if needed. Trim uneven yarn ends and fluff the yarn hair with your fingers to style it.

Yarn Hair Loom

You can easily make long hair from yarn using a simple loom to hold the yarn as you work. The loom can be made small or large to best suit the doll. This method works great when you want to use several colors or textures of yarn at once. Use thick-and-thin yarn, mohair yarn, or sock yarn—better yet, use all three together.

MATERIALS

Measuring tape
Cardboard or plastic foam tray
(a cereal box or bakery tray will
work just fine)
Scissors
Yarn (You will need at least one
4-ounce skein of worsted yarn
to make hair for a doll with a
head that measures 10 inches
around. You'll need more yarn
for larger dolls and less yarn for
smaller ones.)
Needle
Thread to match yarn
Craft glue (optional)

⬤ Decide how long you want the doll's hair to be. Measure that length from the center top of the doll's head. Multiply that number by 2. Cut a square of cardboard or plastic foam that measures that number. For example, if you want the doll's hair to be 4 inches long from the top of the doll's head, multiply 4 inches by 2. Think of it as: 4 × 2 = 8. Then measure and cut a piece of cardboard that is 8 inches across. It can be a square or rectangle.

Cut a piece out of the center of the cardboard. It will create an open area where you can do the stitching to hold the yarn pieces together.

Wrap the yarn around and around the cardboard loom. If you want to use more than one color or type of yarn in the hair, wrap them at the same time, holding them all together as you wrap. Don't pull the yarn too tight as you wrap or the loom will bend and the hair will end up shorter than you wanted. Continue wrapping about 30 rounds. If you end up with too large a wig, you can trim some off later. If you end up needing more wig to cover the doll's head, just make another wig piece.

Now you will stitch the yarn wraps together to hold them in place. Thread a sewing needle with thread to match the yarn. Double the thread and knot the ends. Stitch across the center of the loom, stitching through several yarns at once. Work back over the first row of stitches to be sure all yarn pieces are caught in the stitching. Keep the stitches even and straight across the loom.

Use scissors to cut the yarn strands along both sides of the loom.

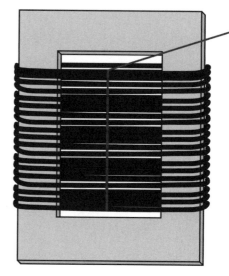

Try the wig on the doll, placing the line of stitches along the center of the head for a center part. If you want a short mop-top hairstyle, place the stitching line across the center top of the head, from ear to ear, letting hair hang to the front and back.

Use a needle and thread to stitch the hair to the head on a cloth doll or use craft glue to fasten the wig to a plastic doll. Sew along the center line of stitching on the wig, then make stitches across the back of the head near the neckline, securing a few strands of yarn to cover the back of the head. Stitch strands of yarn securely over the ears, too. Drape the rest of the strands over to cover the stitching.

Stuffing

For stuffing soft cloth dolls, you can use polyester fiberfill, sold in fabric and craft stores, or clean wool fleece. Polyester fiber stuffing washes easily and is widely available. You can find fiberfill made from corn, soy, and other products that work great, too. Other types of stuffing include scraps of old T-shirts or yarn. If you have discarded pillows, open them up and reuse the clean stuffing. Store stuffing in large plastic bags or old pillowcases closed with rubber bands. If you are using wool fleece stuffing, be sure it has been thoroughly washed and dried, and keep it stored in a closed plastic bag to discourage moths.

The amount of stuffing and how firmly it's used in the body parts can have a real effect on the doll. Less stuffing makes a soft, floppy doll, perfect for a sleepy baby doll, perhaps. More stuffing makes the body parts firm and solid, with stiff arms and legs. That's better for a doll you want to stand up.

Getting the stuffing into the doll body parts is tricky and is key to making a successful doll. Use a dowel or wood chopstick to push small wads of stuffing into hands and feet areas. If you want to push stuffing into narrow body parts, use a pair of long-nose pliers or tweezers. Push pinches of stuffing into the doll parts with the tweezers if your fingers are too large. You can use a toothpick to push stuffing into tiny areas. Leave the tops of legs empty of stuffing, so they can move a bit and the doll can be positioned in a seated pose.

You can adjust the stuffing in the head to show the doll's age. Babies have round heads and faces with thick lower cheeks. Older ages have longer, thinner heads and faces, with noses that stick out more.

You might want to make dolls filled with materials other than fiberfill stuffing. To make a heavy doll, sew a small cloth bag, fill it with dry rice or popcorn kernels, and sew it closed. Tuck the bag into the doll's center or base. Pack stuffing around it before sewing the body together. Other stuffing materials include plastic pellets, kitty litter, clean sawdust, small pebbles (sold in the floral department of craft stores), foam, and plastic foam packing peanuts. It just depends on the kind of doll you want: one to cuddle and play with or one to dress and display.

Hand Stitching

About 150 years ago, the sewing machine was invented. Before that, people stitched everything by hand with a needle and thread. Wedding dresses, work pants, tents, even hot air balloons, ship's sails, and water hoses—all stitched by hand. Women and girls did most of the home sewing, while men—called tailors—set up shops in towns and cities. Wealthy women had dressmakers come to their homes to sew for them. Girls were taught to stitch at a very young age and often earned money sewing for others. Nearly everyone who sewed was also a designer, because there weren't paper patterns. Women studied magazines and fashion dolls dressed in small versions of popular fashions, then sewed copies, adding their own touches.

Sewing by machine is common today, and factories turn out most of the world's clothing. But sewing by hand is still important. Practicing small, careful stitches helps train your eyes, hands, and brain to work together. Hand sewing projects can be taken anywhere, tucked in a backpack or bag. Stitches can be made quietly at night, waking no one in the house. Sewing machines, loud and heavy, have their place, but stitching by hand has many advantages.

Hand sewing requires needles and thread. The best needles to start with are called embroidery needles. They have larger openings, called eyes, to more easily push the thread end through, and they are short so they are easier to handle on small projects. To thread a needle, wet the end of the thread (yep, in your mouth!), then squeeze it flat between your thumb and finger. That will shape it to go through the eye of the needle. Once threaded, pull the thread end to create a knot. Roll a loop twice around your fingertip, rolling the loops together and sliding them off your finger, while pulling it tight into a knot. To sew with regular sewing thread, use a doubled length of thread with both ends knotted together. To sew with embroidery thread, knot only one end and let the other end hang loose as you sew. Adjust the thread length as you work, until you run out of thread.

Some stitchers make knots with the thread when they finish. Another option is to make two or three tiny stitches, one on top of the other, at the end of stitching, then clip the thread next to the last stitch. That will secure the threads without an awkward knot that might unravel later.

Sewing thread comes in many colors and types. Choose polyester or cotton thread for most projects, using the same type of thread for hand sewing or machine sewing. Embroidery thread (also called floss) can be used only for hand sewing and also comes in many colors. It is not sold on spools, like sewing thread, but in small bundles. To use embroidery thread, you need to do some preparation. The thread must be wound on bobbins so it won't tangle. You can buy cardboard or plastic bobbins, but it's very easy to make some for yourself.

Make Bobbins

You can use a Popsicle stick for an embroidery floss bobbin— use one for each color of floss. Or trace and cut bobbin shapes from lightweight cardboard. Here you will learn how to make, load up, and store some cute and useful bobbins.

MATERIALS

Popsicle sticks or cardboard
  (Cereal boxes or egg cartons
  are good sources.)
Permanent markers (Regular
  markers could bleed and stain
  your embroidery floss.)
Scissors
Embroidery thread

⬤ Start with a Popsicle stick, and decorate it with clever designs using permanent markers. If you're making cardboard bobbins, draw and cut out designs. Wind the floss around the bobbin. To keep the thread from unwinding, cut a tiny slit along the edge of the bobbin and secure the loose end of thread in it. Make a different bobbin for each color of thread.

Here are some cute bobbin designs; can you think of more?

If you have plastic photo protective sheets, you can slip bobbins in the pockets to keep them sorted and easy to find.

Hand Stitches to Know

Once your thread is assembled and stored on bobbins, you're ready to stitch. There are lots of stitches, each with its own name and purpose. Maybe you will invent one of your own. Meanwhile, you only need to know three stitches to make lots of handmade projects. And, if you want to decorate your doll or clothing with embroidery, you'll want to know a fourth, the satin stitch.

RUNNING STITCH

Make long, straight stitches, going from front to back. They can be tiny and close together to hold a seam or longer so they can be pulled tight to wrinkle the fabric into gathers.

BLANKET STITCH

This stitch is perfect for edgings—it was created to use around the edges of blankets. It keeps the edges from curling up or unraveling. It also looks cool as a decorative finish.
Be sure to keep the stitches all the same as you work, because they will be visible on the outside of the garment.

LADDER STITCH

This one stitches two pieces together. Use the needle to pull a stitch in one piece, then into the other, as you continue down the seam. It's perfect to stitch heads onto doll bodies. Be sure to go around the neck at least twice to secure it. Ladder stitch is usually hidden from view.
If done properly, you won't even see the stitches.

SATIN STITCH

The satin stitch doesn't sew seams; it's for decorating with embroidery thread. You make small straight stitches right next to each other, to fill in a section. It is perfect for embroidering eyes and mouths on dolls and toys. Eyes done with satin stitch won't smear, get torn off, or be a hazard to a baby.

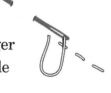

Dolls

You can make dolls that look like people or crazy made-up creatures. Dolls can be works of art, or they can be toys. A lively, clever doll can be appealing because it's unusual and unique. It shows the idea of a person—not an actual person. Think of your favorite cartoons and animated film characters. They may not be very real looking, but they give you an idea of their personality.

Before dolls could be easily purchased in stores, mothers made dolls for their children to keep them busy and happy. Every doll was different. Some mothers made fancier, more complicated dolls, while others made a simple bundle with a face. Today children's toy dolls are inexpensive and easy to find. Few people make dolls unless they want to enjoy being creative and artistic. Some adults are full-time professional doll artists. They make finely crafted dolls that are exhibited in art galleries and sold to collectors around the world. You may start making a few dolls for yourself to enjoy and eventually decide to expand your effort, becoming a doll artist.

The National Institute of American Doll Artists (NIADA) is an organization for professional doll makers who create original dolls of very high quality. The group meets for annual conventions and holds workshops and competitions for doll makers. To join, a doll maker's work must be deemed high quality by other artist members. Visit the website at www.niada.org.

Doll artists enjoy studying people. They like working with fabric, paint, clay, and other art materials
to make a small creature that comes to life with a
personality of its own. You'll use materials and an
idea to come up with something that is totally
one of a kind—just like you. Your doll will
be something that did not exist before.
Give it a name and a story, then craft
a world for it with clothing, houses,
and adventures.

Gingerbread Dolls

Long ago, small dolls made of baked gingerbread were sold at country fairs and celebrations, and most everyone could afford to enjoy them. It is said that Queen Elizabeth I of England introduced them at a party where she served cookies made to look like her guests. Today we still enjoy gingerbread cookies during the Christmas holidays.

Here's a traditional recipe you can use to make a batch of gingerbread dolls.

ADULT SUPERVISION REQUIRED

INGREDIENTS

½ cup sugar
½ cup cooking oil or shortening
½ cup dark molasses
¼ cup water
½ teaspoon salt
½ teaspoon ground ginger
½ teaspoon ground cinnamon
½ teaspoon baking soda
2¾ cups flour, plus extra for board

UTENSILS

Measuring cups and spoons
Mixing bowl
Mixing spoon
Cutting board (optional)
Rolling pin (optional)
Cookie cutter (optional)
Baking sheet
Icing in various colors

● Preheat the oven to 375 degrees.
Combine the ingredients, using a mixing spoon or your hands to work the dough until it's smooth and evenly blended.

Sprinkle flour on the counter or a cutting board and on a rolling pin, to keep the dough from sticking. Roll out the dough till it's about ¼ inch thick. Use gingerbread boy or girl cookie cutters to cut out figures. Gently lay them on an ungreased baking sheet. You can also roll the dough into small balls with your hands, then press the pieces together on the baking sheet to make doll figures. Bake for 8 to 10 minutes.

You can use decorator icing, sold in squeeze tubes in the baking section of the grocery store, to decorate the dolls when they are cooled.

PAPER DOLLS

Paper dolls can be made for playing or for display on a desk or wall. You can spend a lot of time on them and store them carefully in a flat box, or just work quickly, making simple dolls, then toss them when you are bored and replace them with new ones.

Paper dolls have been around for about 200 years; before that, paper and paints weren't available to most children. Magazines used to feature paper dolls printed for children to color with crayons and then cut out. As comic books became popular, they often featured paper doll characters. Today, you can practice drawing a comic character before creating your own unique designs.

There are two basic types of paper doll: the folded chain of identical dolls and the separately drawn and cutout doll with clothing attached by tabs.

Paper Doll Chain

Here's a quick way to make several doll shapes that are all identical. Add details to each one to make them unique, or make them all alike—it's up to you. You can keep them linked in a chain or separate them by clipping them apart at the hands and feet.

MATERIALS

Drawing or copy paper, about 8½ by 11 inches

Scissors

Pencil with eraser

Gingerbread boy cookie cutter (optional)

Pens, crayons, or colored pencils (optional)

● Fold the paper in half lengthwise, then open it and cut along the fold, making two pieces, each measuring 4¼ by 11 inches.

11"

4¼"

Fold each piece in half widthwise, then in half widthwise again.

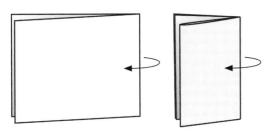

Draw a doll body outline on the folded paper. If you want, you can trace around a cookie cutter. Place the hands and feet on the folds, so they will stay attached when you open up the chain.

Cut out the doll, cutting through all four layers of paper at once. Do not cut open the folds at the hands and feet. Unfold the strip of four doll bodies. Draw on faces and details and color in with crayons if you want.

If you want to make each look a bit different, yet all holding hands, draw and cut out separate heads, then glue to the front of each doll. You can glue on yarn hair or pieces of lace or glitter, too.

Continue making strips of dolls, taping them together until you have a chain as long as you like.

Paper Doll and Wardrobe

It's fun to draw paper dolls. All you need is some scrap paper and a pencil. Drawing your own paper dolls is a lot like being a fashion designer, because you design a wardrobe for the doll. You can also work out designs for cloth or clay dolls by first creating a paper doll version.

MATERIALS

Paper
Pencil with eraser
Permanent marker
Pens, crayons, or colored pencils
Scissors
Card stock (thin cardboard)
White glue or rubber cement

⬤ Use a pencil to sketch a simple doll shape on the paper. (Hint: drawing the feet on a patch of ground, shown here, keeps the feet from curling up or tearing off, and can be detailed to suit the outfit.) Make any changes you want; then go over the pencil lines with permanent marker. Color the details of hair, face, and under-wear; then cut out the doll along the outlined edge. Lay the doll right side up on the card stock and trace around the outer edge. Apply white school glue or rubber cement to the card stock inside the outline. Gently press the doll into the glue and smooth out all the wrinkles. Let dry. Cut out the doll around the edges.

Now you're ready to make a wardrobe. Lay the cutout doll on a blank sheet of paper; then lightly trace around the body. Remove the doll and draw an outfit inside the outline. Draw tabs at the shoulders, legs, and base, each about ½ inch long. Color the outfit, then cut it out along the outline, cutting around the tabs, too. Fold the tabs to hold the clothing on the doll.

Dancing Paper Doll

Dolls with jointed arms and legs, called jumping jacks, were a big hit in Europe about 300 years ago. Made from wood and hand painted, they were children's toys, but adults enjoyed them too. Some were painted to look like famous people and poke fun at the celebrities of the day. People also bought jumping jack kits, to paint and put together at home. They were a very popular adult toy in France until they were outlawed because some fearful people claimed women who played with them might give birth to children with disabilities. That wasn't true, of course, but from then on they were just sold as children's toys.

To make a jumping jack, you can draw your own face or cut out faces from newspapers and magazines. Try using a photograph of yourself, trimmed to fit the paper doll's head.

MATERIALS

White card stock or heavy paper
Pens, crayons, or colored pencils
Scissors
Hole punch
6 brass brads (sold in the office
   supply section of stores)

◉ Use the pattern or come up with your own design for the jumping jack. Draw or trace the doll's head, torso, two arms, and two legs. Draw and color in details like a facial expression, hairstyle, and clothing. Cut out all the pieces.

Punch a hole in the top of each arm and a hole at both shoulders on the torso piece. Push the pointed end of a brad through the hole in the arm, then through the hole in the torso. Open the arms of the brad, pressing them flat against the back of the torso. Attach the other arm and both legs with brads.

Wiggle the arms and legs—they should move freely. If not, make the holes a bit larger or loosen the brads a bit.

If you want to create dolls that move at the elbow, wrist, knee, and ankle, just make all the pieces, then attach with brads at each joint.

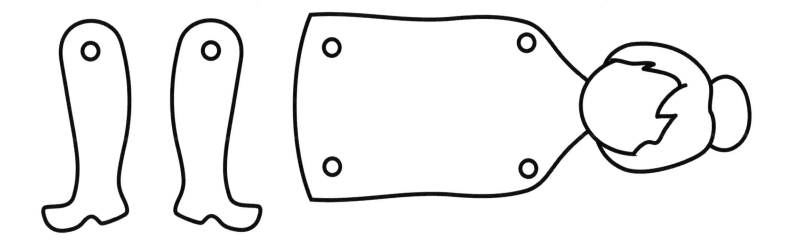
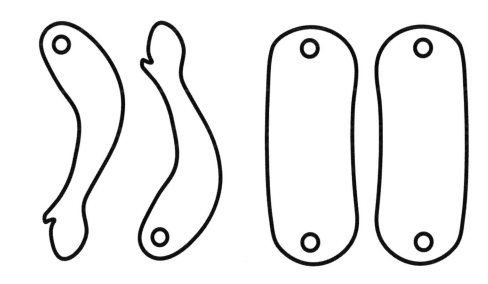

Selfie Paper Doll

Make a paper doll from your own photo—a little "mini-me" or doppelgänger.

ADULT SUPERVISION REQUIRED

MATERIALS

Photo of yourself (or whoever you want to make a doll for)
Scissors
White glue or rubber cement
Foam-core poster board
Craft knife (be careful—ask an adult for help)
Sandpaper or nail file (optional)
Drawing paper
Pens, crayons, or colored pencils
Manila file folder

⬤ Use a full-body photo. Pose in a swimsuit or tank top and shorts, so you can make a wardrobe for the doll. Take the photo to a copy shop and have it enlarged to 8 to 10 inches tall and printed in color (or black and white if you want to color it in with pens, crayons, or pencils).

Trim around the figure with scissors. Glue it to a piece of foam-core poster board. Smooth out all the wrinkles gently with your fingertips. Let dry. With adult help, use a craft knife to cut through the foam board around the image. Be careful—the craft knife is very sharp. Smooth out rough edges with sandpaper or a nail file if necessary.

Now you're ready to draw a wardrobe of clothes and accessories. Trace around the doll's outline on drawing paper, then draw, color, and cut out garments to wear. Draw tabs at the shoulders of the outfits to hold in place on the doll.

If you want to display the selfie paper doll, glue an easel back to the figure. Cut a strip of foam-core board and fold back one end about 1 inch to make a tab. Position the tab on the back of the doll and glue in place. Extend the other end of the strip back, to balance the doll.

Next, make a backdrop—like a little room—for your paper doll. Open a manila file folder. Draw windows and doors, color some wallpaper, add furniture—make whatever scene you want your doll to live in. When open, the backdrop will stand on a tabletop, so the doll can enjoy shopping, her bedroom, or even a castle setting.

Gymnast Doll

It's fascinating to build auto-matons—figures that move automatically—so here's a simple paper doll gymnast that can actually climb tiny ropes!

MATERIALS

Heavy drawing paper
Pen or pencil
Markers or crayons
Glitter (optional)
Scissors
Drinking straw
Craft glue
Measuring tape or ruler
Tape
Hole punch
Yarn
2 craft beads or safety pins large enough so they won't slip through the straw opening

◉ Draw a figure or copy the one here. Color and decorate it, even adding glitter if you want. Cut it out. Cut two pieces each about 1 inch long from the drinking straw. Glue the straw pieces to the back of the doll, laying them flat behind the arm area, placing them so the top ends are slightly angled inward, as shown.

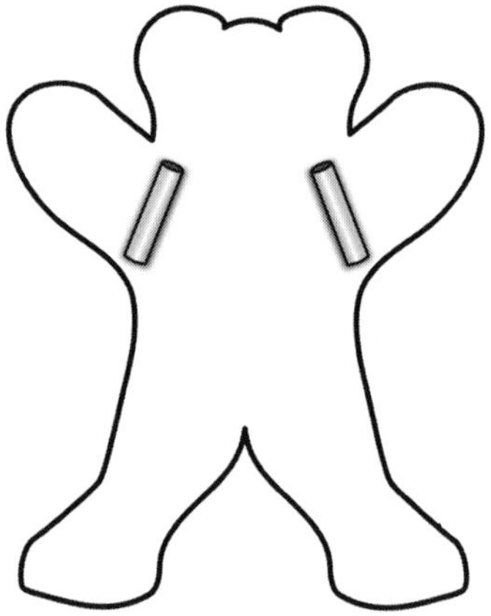

Make a handle to operate the toy. Cut a rectangle of paper, about 4 inches by 6 inches. Fold it lengthwise twice and tape to hold it. Use a hole punch to punch a hole about ½ inch from each end. Punch a third hole in the center.

Cut a piece of yarn about 10 inches long and thread it through the center hole of the handle, tying the ends in a knot. This will be a hanging loop you can attach to a nail, hook, or doorknob.

Cut another piece of yarn about 48 inches long. Slip the ends through the holes at the ends of the handle. Thread the ends through the straws on the back of the doll. Tie a bead or safety pin to the bottom of both yarn ends, so they won't slide back out through the straws.

Now you're ready to operate the gymnast—hang the loop from a hook and gently pull one side of the string, then the other, and your doll will magically climb the ropes.

Beginning of Robots

Automatons, or dolls that could move, were the beginnings of today's robots. The earliest were made by the ancient Greeks, who created statues and figures that appeared to move, and displayed them in temples. People thought they were spirits and made pilgrimages to see them, leaving generous offerings. Centuries later, during the 1700s, inventors created dolls that could move, called automatons. They were handmade and expensive but provided great entertainment for adults. Remember, there was no television that long ago, so automatons were very popular at parties.

Some automaton dolls played musical instruments: one played 18 different songs on the harpsichord (like a keyboard), and another even blew air into a flute to make music. One doll sat at a desk and wrote with a feather quill pen, marking over a hundred words at a time. Windup dolls that moved on wheels hidden beneath long skirts appeared to walk across a room. There was even a swimming doll. It had a body made of cork so it stayed afloat while a windup device moved the arms and legs.

Clothespin Doll

Today, clothespins are made with metal springs to hold the pieces together. To make these clothespin dolls, you'll need to find the old-fashioned type made of one piece of wood that just slips onto the clothesline. Those pins are sold in craft stores in the wood crafts department.

MATERIALS

Wooden clothespins for crafts (not the kind with metal springs)
Fine-tip markers or pens
Fabric, felt, yarn, and paper scraps
Scissors
Glue
Modeling clay (optional)

⬤ Draw faces and hair on the clothespins with pens or markers. You can color the body and feet with different colors and patterns, using the pens, or make clothing from fabric and felt scraps. Keep the clothing simple. Cut a rectangle for a tunic or top, making a hole in the center to slip the head

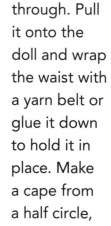

through. Pull it onto the doll and wrap the waist with a yarn belt or glue it down to hold it in place. Make a cape from a half circle, then fasten the front at the neck with yarn ties or glue. Make a skirt from a half circle wrapped around the waist and glued in place. A square can become a poncho, with a hole cut for a head. Wrap and glue a piece of wide lace around the waistline for a frilly skirt or tutu. To make a doll stand, roll a ball of clay and push the clothespin ends into the clay.

Silly Spoon Doll

Spoon dolls are easy to make and can be held by the handle so they are like puppets. Use large wooden mixing spoons or small—even tiny—snack spoons. Make a whole family, with different sizes of spoons.

MATERIALS

Fabric scraps

Scissors

Wooden spoons or plastic spoons

Rubber bands

Permanent markers

Glue (optional)

Moss, yarn, or wool for hair (optional)

● Cut a piece of fabric long enough to cover the spoon handle, with about an inch extra. Scrunch the cloth around the doll's neck (the top of the spoon handle), with the skirt upside down covering the face (the spoon). Wrap the fabric in place and hold it with a tight rubber band.

Pull the fabric down over the rubber band and adjust it to be the dress. Use markers to draw on the doll's face. Draw or paint on hair—or glue on yarn, moss, or wool.

Handkerchief Doll

No sewing—and very few supplies—are needed to make this "starter doll." It's so easy you'll want to make a basketful of little cuties.

MATERIALS

Handkerchief, cloth napkin, or fabric square
Stuffing (fiberfill, wool, or yarn clippings)
Rubber bands or yarn
Fine-tip marker (optional)

◉ Lay the cloth flat. Pull the corners into knots. Wad the stuffing into a ball and place it in the center of the upper half of the cloth.

Wrap the cloth over the stuffing to create a head and fasten at the neck with rubber bands or a yarn tie. Leave it as is or use a fine-tip marker to draw on a face.

FOLK DOLLS

Simple dolls have always been made from things people found around them: sticks, stones, clay, fiber—whatever was at hand. Today, you can still make traditional dolls that are like those made centuries ago. If you cannot find natural materials, substitute something you find in your own environment—recycled objects work great.

Corn Husk Doll

Where to get corn husks? If you eat fresh corn, save the husks and let them air dry. Dry corn husks are sold in the Mexican foods section of grocery stores. You can also use sheets of folded newspaper, felt, or cloth instead of corn husks to make a folded and wrapped doll.

MATERIALS

5 corn husks

Yarn or string

Scissors

Markers or paints (optional)

Glue

Corn silk, moss, yarn, or wool for hair

◉ Lay four large husks on top of each other. Fold them together in the center. Use a piece of yarn or string to tie a neck about 1 inch below the fold. That will make the head.

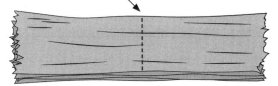
stack, then fold 4 husks in the middle

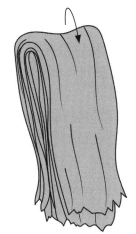

tie a string 1 inch below the fold to make the head

Slip the arm section up inside the neck. Tie yarn tightly below the arms to hold them in place and make a waist. If you want the doll to wear pants, cut the bottom of the husks up to the waist, then tie each side with yarn about

½ inch from the bottom to make the ankles and feet.

If you want to add a face, draw or paint one. Glue on some corn silk, moss, yarn, or wool for hair.

slide the arms up to the neck

tie at the waist

Roll another husk lengthwise to make a long tube. This will be the arms. Tie the ends, about ½ inch from the edges. That will make wrists and hands.

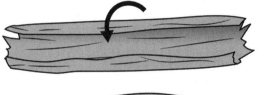

roll 1 cornhusk and tie it at the ends to make arms and hands

Scarecrows?

Did you ever think of a scarecrow as a doll? Well, it is! Scarecrows are part of the tradition of using dolls to scare off spirits or to bring good luck. When autumn comes around and scarecrows are on the scene, add one to your doll collection.

You might also think of a snowman as a doll. A doll can be made of just about anything, after all. Can you think of other kinds of dolls?

Apple Head Doll

Dolls made of foods have a long history—probably because food was always at hand and people like to make clever dolls from just about anything! Apples work well if you want to create an aged-looking doll. The fruit will wrinkle and darken as it dries, creating unique figures with real personality.

ADULT SUPERVISION REQUIRED

MATERIALS

Apple, peeled

Knife or spoon to use as a carving tool

1 cup water

1 tablespoon lemon juice or vinegar

Paints or markers

Craft glue

Natural items for features: cloves, seeds, popcorn kernels, dry rice

Long-necked plastic bottle

Bandana, handkerchief, or other cloth scrap

Hot glue

Pipe cleaners

⦿ It's a good idea to make several of these so you can select the face that you like the best, once the apple has dried and wrinkled. To begin, ask an adult to help you peel a fresh apple, keeping the surface as smooth as you can. Carve a face with a knife, spoon, or other tool. Make a nose and mouth, and carve out eye sockets where the eyes will go later.

Dip the apple in an acidic mixture of 1 cup of water and 1 tablespoon of lemon juice or vinegar. The acid wash will keep the apple from turning too dark as it dries. If you want a darker flesh tone, just let it dry naturally, without the acid wash. It will take a couple of weeks to dry completely.

When it's dried, color the features with paints or markers. You can apply color to the cheeks. Glue something dark and round in the eye sockets for eyes, such as whole cloves, seeds, or popcorn kernels. You can stick in a row of teeth made with seeds, corn, or dry rice, using craft glue to hold them in place if needed.

Use a long-necked bottle as the body. Wrap cloth over the bottle and secure with a rubber band. Use hot glue to secure the apple head in place.

You can also make a body from twisted pipe cleaners, inserting one end into the dry apple for the neck, then wrapping cloth strips around the pipe cleaners until it looks the way you want.

Radish Dolls in Mexico

Every year on December 23, the city of Oaxaca, Mexico, holds a one-day radish carving contest, called Night of the Radishes, to celebrate the Christmas holiday. Radishes are carved and assembled into all kinds of scenes, and radish dolls are the main feature. The carvers use knives and toothpicks to shape their creations, as viewers wait hours in line to see the clever arts. It's all over in one day, though, because fresh radishes don't last long.

Yarn Doll

Here's a simple doll that uses yarn in the wrapping and tying style of the corn husk doll. Add some of these to your doll maker's collection, too.

MATERIALS

Yarn, about 6 yards
Cardboard rectangle, 6 by 8 inches or 4 by 6 inches
Scissors
Felt scraps
Glue or needle and thread

⚫ Make the body by winding yarn 20 times lengthwise around the cardboard. Cut one 4-inch piece of yarn and slip it under the loops at one end. Pull tight and tie a knot to hold the loops together. Slide the loops off the cardboard.

Make the head by cutting a 4-inch piece of yarn and wrapping it around the body loops, about 1 inch from the ends, to create a neck. Pull tight and knot. Roll yarn scraps into a small ball and hide it inside the head section to fill it out and give it a plumper shape.

Make the arms: wind yarn around the cardboard 10 times widthwise, to make shorter loops than for the body. Cut two pieces of yarn about 4 inches long. Slip each piece through the loops at the side of the cardboard. Slide the loops off the cardboard, then pull the yarn pieces tight and tie in a knot. Knot both ends to create the hands.

Slip the arm section in between the body loops, push it up against the neck, and tie a piece of yarn tightly below the arm section to create the waist. Wrap yarn across the chest over the shoulders, to hold the arms in place and better shape the chest. Knot securely and tuck yarn ends inside the doll body to hide.

To make a doll in a skirt, cut through the ends of the loops at the bottom of the body. If you want a doll wearing pants, divide the skirt yarns into two equal sections and tie yarn around the lower ends to make ankles. Trim any yarn ends that are uneven.

Make simple clothes using scraps of felt. You can either glue the clothing in place or sew with a needle and thread.

A simple apron ties at the waist. Use a felt strip or yarn to tie. Glue on or paint a heart or other decoration if you wish.

Use felt to make a little vest that buttons at the front. Cut slits for armholes and the buttonhole.

Worry Doll

Tiny dolls made in Guatemala and Mexico are said to take away a person's fears and worries if placed under a pillow at night. They are made by winding string or yarn around a little body and gluing on hair or clothing. Here are two ways to make them, one with cardboard strips, the other with a wired body so they can be moved into different poses. Make them as tiny or big as you want, then let them do the worrying for you! When they are full of your fears and worries, toss them away. You can always make new ones if you want.

MATERIALS

Cardboard (use a lid from an egg carton or cereal box)
Measuring tape or ruler
Scissors
Embroidery thread or thin yarn in several colors
Pen
Yarn needle
Pipe cleaners
Craft glue
Tiny felt or fabric scraps for clothing

● Cut two cardboard strips, one 2 inches long and ¼ inch wide, the other 2½ inches long and ½ inch wide. Make a slit up the center of the longer one for the legs. Lay the shorter strip across the longer one to create arms. Wrap the doll with embroidery thread or thin yarn, changing colors and wrapping over one section to another. Leave the hands and feet unwrapped. You can leave the head unwrapped, too, and draw features with a pen.

2"

2½"

When you finish wrapping, clip the yarn or thread and leave a 6-inch tail. Thread it onto a yarn needle and stitch into the body two times, then cut the end and hide it inside the body.

To make a worry doll with a wire body that can be moved and posed, use a 5-inch-long pipe cleaner for the body. Fold it in half, with a loop at the center for the head. Twist it once at the neck to hold the shape.

Slip a 4-inch pipe cleaner between the body wires to make the arms, and fold the ends of the arms into the chest so the sharp wire ends will be wrapped and covered. Twist the two leg pieces below the arm piece to secure.

Fold up about ¼ inch at the feet. Wrap the doll with yarn, changing colors for clothing and the head. Bend the hands and feet a bit to keep the yarn from sliding off. Finish by threading the working yarn or thread onto a yarn needle, taking two stitches into the body, then clipping the end of the thread.

Cut tiny scraps of fabric or felt to make clothing and glue it onto the doll body to secure. Hold it securely with your fingers until the glue dries a bit.

Healing Doll

Healing dolls are believed to bring comfort and happiness to someone who needs it. You can make a special doll for someone who is having bad luck or trouble with friends or family. Simply having one nearby can sometimes make people feel better.

Any doll can be a healing doll, but here is how to create one for yourself or a special person you know. A healing doll should be soft and small enough to hold in your hand. No need for much detail—and no wardrobe changes are necessary. Create the doll from materials and colors the owner will enjoy. While you are working on it, keep pleasant thoughts in mind, so the doll will have hope and joy sewn into it.

MATERIALS

Scrap paper and pencil

Stuffing

Fabric square in a flesh color (a piece about 9 by 9 inches makes a 6-inch-tall doll)

Rubber band

Scissors

Yarn

Decorations: buttons, bells, tiny flowers, ribbons, shells, or charms

Fine-tip marker (optional)

● On a scrap of paper, write the wish, dream, or goal you want the doll to work on. It might be joy, strength, friendship, confidence—whatever you choose. Wad up the paper and cover with stuffing, making a ball the size of a Ping-Pong ball. Put it in the center of the fabric square and fold the fabric evenly around the ball, fastening tight around the neck with a rubber band.

Lay the fabric square flat and cut two slits, one on each side, for arms.

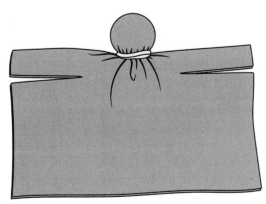

Wrap yarn around the folded fabric arms and around the neck. Crisscross yarn over and around the chest to the waist. Stop here if your doll will have a skirt. For legs, cut a slit down the middle

and divide the skirt fabric in two sections and continue wrapping to the feet. When the doll's body is completely wrapped with yarn, cut the end. Slip the yarn through a loop and pull to make a slipknot. Cut the end and tuck it into the yarn loops to hide it.

Add as many details and decorations as you want. Use a fine-tip marker to draw on a face, or leave it blank.

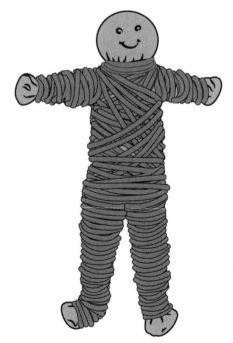

Japanese Doll Festival

Dolls are an important part of Japanese culture. In Japan, Hina Matsuri, or Girls' Day Festival, is held each year. In ancient Japan, dolls were thought to bring good luck. Parents placed them at their child's bedside at night, to protect the child from evil spirits. As the children grew older, the dolls were just toys. Fighting warriors, *samurai*, tied small warrior dolls to their helmets before battle. These dolls, called *musha*, were mascots to bring luck. When important visitors met with the emperor at the palace, they brought gift dolls, *gosho*, to wish good luck to the ruler.

Each year, straw dolls were sent floating down a river to take away the evil spirits from the community. This ritual became the Girls' Day Festival, which is now held on the third day of the third month: March 3.

Voodoo Doll

In Europe, dolls have been used for centuries to fend off bad luck and witches. People thought that if a witch had cast a spell on them, they could get rid of the spell by making a magical doll and sticking pins into it. Those dolls were called voodoo dolls, and they eventually became popular in other parts of the world. A voodoo doll is meant to be discarded once it is no longer useful, so it can be made of just rags or scraps, because it won't be cherished and played with.

MATERIALS

Scissors
Fabric and yarn scraps
Stuffing or cut-up scraps of fabric
Needle and thread or glue
   (optional)
Markers for the face

⊙ You have total freedom to make a voodoo doll any way you want, because there isn't a standard form or design. Just cut some fabric into strips, then roll one strip to create a body and another for arms. Make a head by tying around the neck with a piece of yarn. Insert the arm section beneath the neck and tie it in place, creating a waistline.

Stuff the head and chest area to give the doll more shape. Draw a face and sew or glue on yarn or stuffing for hair. Make the doll look mean and ugly, because it is supposed to scare the bad spirits away.

String Doll

String dolls have become popular in Asia, and their popularity is spreading. There are several stop-motion videos made with string dolls on the Internet. String dolls can be just about any size, shape, or color. Plus, they don't usually have faces—except maybe eyes—so you can just keep yours simple.

MATERIALS

18 inches of 20-gauge copper craft wire

1- or 2-inch Styrofoam ball

Thin knitting needle or wooden skewer (optional)

Pliers

Yarn or string

Scissors

◉ Poke one end of the wire straight through the foam ball and out the other end. If you have trouble getting it through the foam, use a thin knitting needle or wooden skewer to poke a hole first. Pull the wire through until the ball sits in the center of the 18 inches of wire. Bend the two ends of wire around the ball until they meet just beneath the ball, then twist them together firmly to create the doll's neck.

Use pliers to bend the wires into loops to create arms, then twist at the waist a couple of times to create the torso. Turn up the sharp ends of the wire for each foot.

Begin wrapping yarn or string tightly around the neck, then go over the head until the ball is completely covered. Keep the yarn tight as you work. Wrap the arms, torso, and each leg.

When you are done and the doll is as chubby as you want, clip the yarn end and slip it through a loop, pulling tight to create a slipknot.

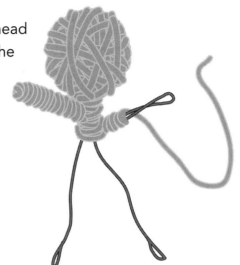

Islam and Dolls

Islamic religious doctrine prohibits artwork or crafts that depict facial features, whether animal or human. Some Muslim children are allowed to play with dolls, but as they grow older they must avoid them.

Stick Doll

These are very creative dolls and make clever wall decorations. Just prop them on a shelf so they can keep you company.

MATERIALS

Heavy paper: white and various colors

Colored pencils, pens, or crayons

Scissors

Craft glue

2 twigs, the same length, at least 6 inches long

Buttons, ribbons, or other trimmings

⬤ Draw on paper a head and face and a pair of hands as shown. Color the features, then cut them out.

Use a rectangle-shaped piece of paper in any color to make the body. Fold it in thirds widthwise. Squirt a line of glue along the inside of the folds. Lay the twigs inside the folds on top of the glue.

Fold the paper over the twigs, pressing to be sure the glue holds.

Now you have the body—the twigs stick out at the top and bottom for arms and legs. Glue colored paper, buttons, and trim to the front of the doll body. Last, glue the cutout head onto the body at the shoulders and the hands at the ends of the arms. If you want to add details, just cut out and glue on paper feet, shoes, mittens (from felt, perhaps), or whatever you can think of.

Pocket Gnome

You can make tons of these tiny dolls. Dress them as gnomes, trolls, elves, or just sleeping babies. Use the patterns here, then make some tinier ones or larger ones by changing the size of the pattern pieces.

MATERIALS

Paper and pencil

Felt scraps

Scissors

Jar lid or drinking glass, 3 to 4 inches across

Sock or nylon stocking (you can make three or four gnomes from one sock)

Needle and embroidery thread

Stuffing

Sewing pins

● Trace the pattern pieces onto paper and use them to cut out two felt body pieces (a front and a back) and one hat piece.

Make a head pattern by tracing a circle around a jar lid or drinking glass that measures 3 to 4 inches across. Use that pattern to cut out one circle head shape from a sock or nylon stocking.

Make the head first. With needle and thread, sew running stitches around the edge of the circle. Roll a ball of stuffing about the size of a golf ball or Ping-Pong ball. Press it firmly.

You can adjust the amount of stuffing to make the head smaller or larger. Place the stuffing in the center of the head circle and pull the stitching tight so the circle wraps around the stuffing. Pull tight and make three tiny stitches to secure the thread. Clip the thread.

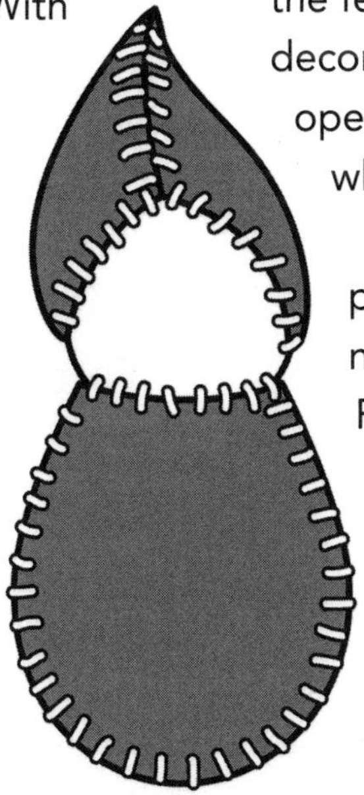

Make the body. A second body style is shown here. Sew the front and back together around the outside edges using the blanket stitch. You can use thread to match the felt or a contrasting color for decoration. Be sure to leave an opening at the neck no matter which body style you choose.

Stuff the body lightly then position the head with the neck down inside the opening. Pin it in place, then stitch the body to the head all around.

Stitch the sides of the hat together. Position the hat on the head and stitch it in place all around.

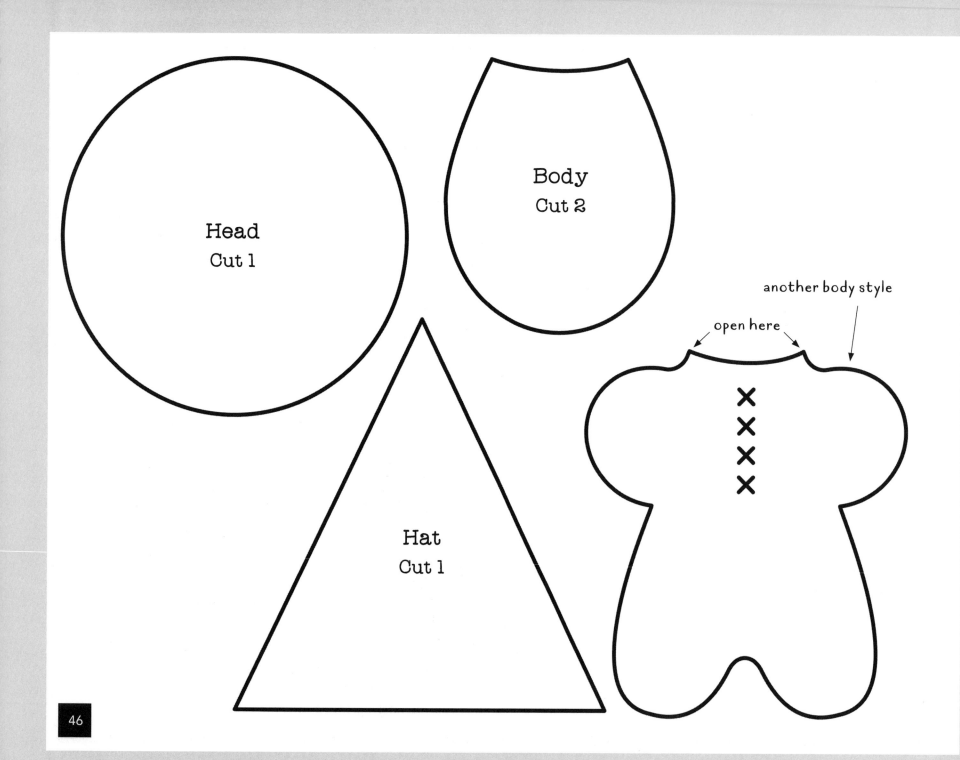

Head
Cut 1

Body
Cut 2

another body style

open here

Hat
Cut 1

You can add extras, like a wool or yarn beard for a gnome or a felt strip wrapped around the neck for a scarf.

Matryoshka Nesting Dolls

Traditional dolls from Russia, called matryoshka, are sets of dolls made to nest inside each other. They are carved from wood and painted bright colors. The smallest is the baby, and the largest is the grandmother.

SOCK DOLLS

Socks make great dolls because they are soft, washable, stretchy, and easy to find. You can make dolls that are just simple sleeping babies or very complicated ones. Every sock doll will look unique just by the way it is stuffed and the personality you give it. Socks also make great doll clothing, too. (Check out the projects in the Doll Clothes and Accessories section of this book beginning on page 87.) Start saving socks that have lost their partners and give them new life as dolls!

You may want to color white socks in a variety of flesh tones. You can make up several at once to have on hand for craft days. All-cotton or cotton blend socks work best. Acrylic or polyester won't dye easily. Use a mug of hot water and a tea bag or teaspoon of instant coffee. Let the tea or coffee sit a few minutes. Wet the sock in water first, then dip it into the mug of tea or coffee and pull it out to check how dark the color is. Leave it in longer for a darker color. When it's as dark as you like, squeeze out the moisture by rolling the sock in a towel. Let it dry before beginning crafting.

Soft Sock Baby Doll

This is a stuffed cloth doll that takes no sewing. Because sock sizes and stretchiness vary, you will see different results using different socks. Experiment!

MATERIALS

1 sock (sport socks with ribbed cuffs work best)
Stuffing (polyester or wool)
2 rubber bands or yarn
Scissors

⦿ Start with the head: push a few handfuls of stuffing into the toe of the sock and fasten tightly with a rubber band or yarn. Make the body: stuff half the sock, then fasten with a rubber band or yarn. Roll the remaining portion of the sock (the part with the ribbed cuff) up and over the body and fold it around the neck. Make a hat from another sock by cutting across the sock a bit below the cuff. Turn it inside out and fasten the cut end tightly with a rubber band. Turn right side out and stretch to fit over the doll's head. The cute little baby is tucked in for a nap.

Soft Sculpture Sock Doll

If you want to do some stitching, take the sock doll a bit further with this project. You'll use a needle and thread to do the "sculpture" details.

MATERIALS

1 sock (sport socks with ribbed
   cuffs work best)
Stuffing (polyester or wool)
3 rubber bands or yarn
Needle
Sewing thread to match the sock
Scissors
Pencil
Embroidery thread for eyes and
   mouth
Pink crayon or makeup blusher
   (optional)

◉ Begin by stuffing the entire sock, from the toe to the ribbing on the cuff. Position the neck about a third of the way down from the cuff. The other two-thirds of the sock will be the body section. Use a rubber band or yarn tie to make the neck. Fasten another at the top of the head. The cuff section will be a cap.

   Use a large needle and matching thread to stitch down the center of the body to create legs. Stitch through the body from front to back. Stitch the same way about an inch from the sides, making the arms.

cuff

toe

Use a pencil to make tiny marks where you want the eyes to be. Thread the needle with three strands of embroidery thread, knotted at the end. Insert the threaded needle through the top of the head and pull it out at one of the eye locations. Make several stitches next to each other for the eye, then insert the needle

through the head to come out at the top of the head where you started.

Pull the thread tight so the eye pulls into the head a bit. Make three tiny stitches to hold the thread and clip. Do the same for the other eye. Make the mouth the same way, using a pencil to mark the corners of the mouth, then pulling gently on the thread and securing with a few stitches at the top of the head. Pull the cuff of the sock down onto the head for a cap. You can add a bit of pink crayon or makeup blusher to the cheeks to bring the doll to life. Done!

Advanced Sock Doll

Here's a sock doll with more stitching and body parts—and hair. You can make clothing for her from felt pieces (see the Doll Clothes and Accessories section of this book beginning on page 87 for ideas). Like all sock dolls, the finished size will vary depending on the type and size of socks you use and how much stuffing you put into the doll.

MATERIALS

1 adult size sport sock

Scissors

Needle and thread

Stuffing

Chopstick

Yarn, felt, or other scrap material

2 buttons (optional, for eyes)

Embroidery thread, paint, or fine-tip marker (optional, for face details)

Pink crayon (optional)

◉ Lay the sock flat and cut straight down the center of the ribbed section, cutting through both the front and back at the same time. Cut off half of each section. Those pieces will be the arms. Stitch around two sides of the arm pieces, as shown. You will stuff and stitch them in place on the doll's body later.

Use the larger sock section to make the body. Use strong, tiny stitches to sew the center seam between the legs, but leave the bottom of the legs open for now. Push stuffing into the body through the leg holes, using a chopstick to push it into place.

stitch for arms

stitch for legs

Tie a yarn piece tightly around the end of the stuffed sock to create a neck. Knot it securely. Push the stuffing to shape the doll's body, then tuck the ends of the legs inside and sew closed. Stuff the arm pieces, tuck the raw edges inside, and stitch the arms to the body. Be sure to place the arms so they are positioned evenly on the body.

Make hair from yarn, felt, or cut-up old sweaters. Cut several thin strips as long as you want the hair to be and stitch them to the doll's head. You can make a short bob, long ponytails, or even bangs.

Make the face by sewing on buttons for eyes, or use embroidery thread or paint. You can use fine-tip markers to dot on tiny freckles. Rub a little pink crayon onto the cheeks to add a blush.

Topsy-Turvy Zombie Doll

Topsy-turvy dolls have been around for generations. *They are actually two dolls in one, attached at the middle. A long skirt covers one doll—then flip the skirt and reveal the other doll. A "sleep and wake" doll is fun to make—just flip the skirt and the doll changes from awake to asleep. In another version, one doll is Red Riding Hood and the flip doll is the wolf. You can choose any two characters you like for this project. For fun, you can make a happy doll that flips to a crazy-looking zombie doll. Whatever you choose, be sure the skirt is long enough to cover each doll when it is the one that is hidden.*

MATERIALS

1 tube sock

Scissors

Stuffing

Needle and thread

Yarn, about 20 inches long, plus an extra scrap to create the two heads

Cloth square, 18 by 18 inches (a handkerchief is perfect for this project)

Sewing pins

Materials to decorate the dolls:
felt, yarn, fringe, embroidery thread

Materials to make the faces:
marking pens, embroidery thread, crayons, paints

◉ Cut the cuff off the sock. Stuff the sock, then use a needle and thread to stitch running stitches along the cut end.

Pull the thread to gather the stitches together as tightly as you can. Stitch two or three tiny stitches in one place to hold the thread, then clip the end.

Wrap a piece of scrap yarn around the middle of the stuffed sock a few times, pull it tight, then tie it off with a knot, creating two heads. Trim the yarn end.

Now make a skirt from a square piece of cloth about 18 by 18 inches. Lay the 20-inch piece of yarn along the center of the square, straightening it if needed. Fold the fabric in half over the yarn and line up the edges so they are even all around. Use some sewing pins to hold the fabric and yarn in place while you sew a tube, or casing, with the yarn inside. Use a needle and sewing thread and make short running stitches about one inch from the folded edge. Be careful as you work that you don't get the yarn caught in the stitches. When you've sewn all the way across, make three tiny stitches to hold the thread and clip the ends.

Gently pull the yarn ends, gathering the skirt to fit the doll. Tie it securely around the center of the stuffed sock and fasten with a knot or bow at the back of the doll. Now, whichever doll is showing, the cloth skirt will cover the other one.

Decorate the faces with whatever you have: button eyes, felt scraps, or draw with pen or paint. Create some hair from yarn loops or felt, and glue or sew it in place. Make the zombie doll as weird as you want—felt teeth, horns, or whatever comes to mind.

Now you can tell a story to a friend, acting it out with one doll until the other appears in the story—then switch dolls right before their eyes!

FUN FELT DOLLS

Felt is a perfect material for creating dolls. It doesn't unravel, so you don't have to sew hems. There is no "right" or "wrong" side to the fabric. It comes in lots of colors. And best of all, you can buy felt made from recycled plastic bottles. You can help save the ocean and the planet by making dolls!

Tiny Felt Dolls

These little dolls are quick and easy to make—perfect for a first-time doll maker. They also make cute dolls for your bigger dolls. After all, dolls need dolls, too, don't they? Make a baby doll, a teddy bear, or one of the other dolls shown here.

MATERIALS

Paper and pencil
Scissors
Felt scraps in colors for the face and blanket or body
Needle and matching thread
Sewing pins
Stuffing
Fine-tip markers, brown and red
Other trimmings (optional)

● Use a pencil to draw a body shape like the one shown here. Cut it out to use as a pattern. With a pencil, lightly trace around the pattern onto the felt to make two body pieces that are the same size and shape. Cut them out, and be sure both

stuff then stitch closed

body pieces are the same. Cut a small circle from felt for the doll's face.

Hand stitch the face in place on one of the body pieces, using running stitches.

Lay the body pieces together, matching the edges. Use pins to hold them together so they don't shift as you sew. Use running stitches to sew the back to the front all around the outer seam, leaving the bottom open

for stuffing. Stuff the doll lightly with a few pieces of stuffing, then pin the bottom edges together. Stitch across the bottom with running stitches. Draw a face on the doll with fine-tip markers. Sew or glue on trim, such as yarn hair, lace, ribbon bows, or felt cutouts.

Below are some variations you can try.

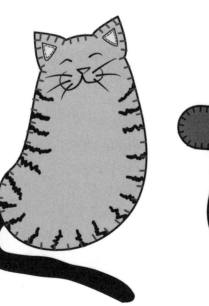

Sassy 10-Inch Felt Doll and Outfit

This 10-inch-tall doll is full of spunk. Use the patterns provided here to make the doll and its clothing from felt, hand stitching the seams on the outside. The hair is felt, too.

MATERIALS

Paper and pencil or copies of the patterns

12-inch felt squares: 4 in flesh tone, 1 in hair color, and additional squares for clothing

Scissors

Needle and embroidery thread

Sewing pins

Sewing thread to match flesh-toned felt

Stuffing

Fabric glue (optional)

Sew-on snap

◉ Using the patterns here, cut out two head pieces, front and back, from a felt square. Use three strands of embroidery thread to stitch the eyes, mouth, nose, and brows on one of the head pieces. Pin the pieces together. Use sewing thread to sew blanket stitches around the edges, leaving about 2 inches open at the neck.

Fold another felt square and lay the body pattern along the folded edge. Cut out two bodies. Pin them together and sew a blanket stitch all around the outside edges. Leave the neck open. Stuff the arms and legs, then sew a line of running stitches across the hip and shoulder. This will allow the doll to move its arms and legs.

Stuff the torso and neck firmly. Stuff the head firmly and pin it onto the neck, tucking the edges inside to hide them.

Sew the head to the neck with a ladder stitch, going around twice so it is firmly attached.

leave open

Cut out the wig pieces from felt and stitch the front and back together along the outer edge.

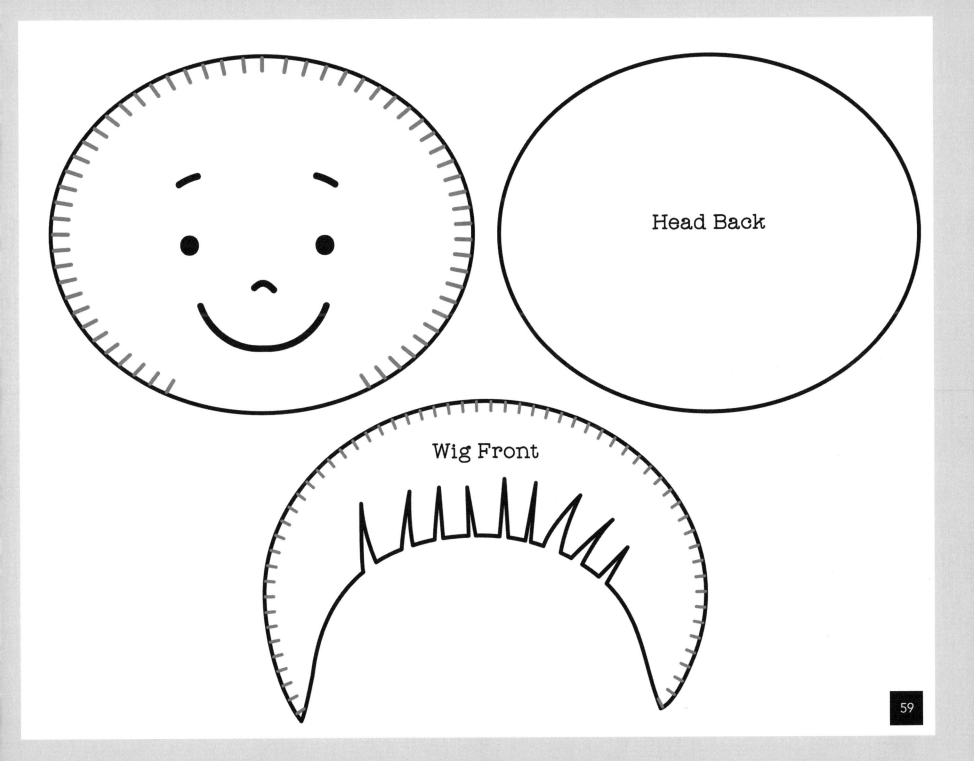

Head Back

Wig Front

59

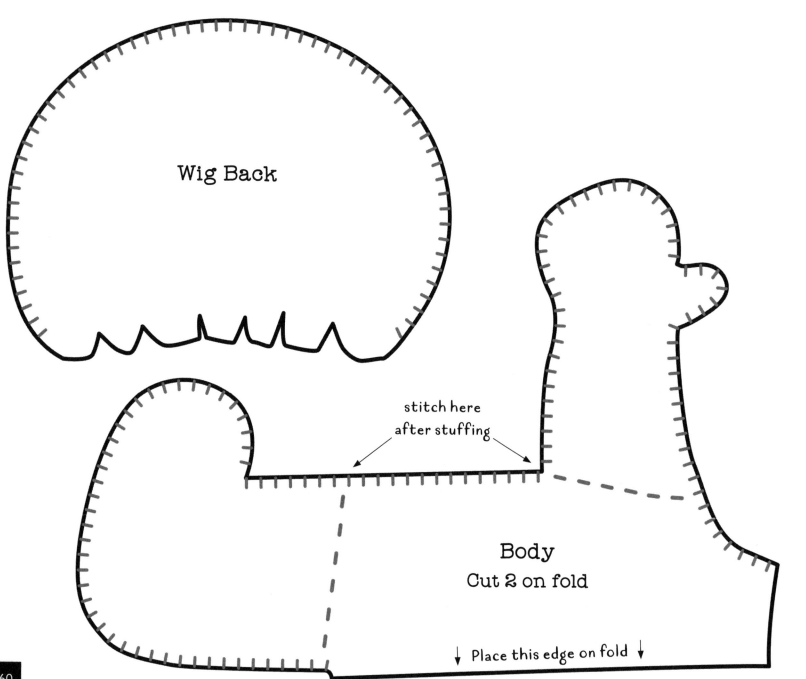

Wig Back

stitch here
after stuffing

Body
Cut 2 on fold

↓ Place this edge on fold ↓

Pin it on the doll's head and sew it in place all around. You can use fabric glue instead, if you choose. If you want ponytails, sew strips of felt to the sides of the head. Braid thin strips and sew in place for braids.

Panties or Shorts

Cut panties or shorts using the pattern provided, then fold them and stitch the edges as shown.

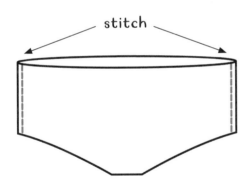

stitch

Top or Dress

Make a top or dress from the patterns shown on pages 63–64. Cut one front and one back piece. Stitch the sides together, using a blanket stitch and three strands of embroidery thread, making sure to leave the armholes open. Sew a snap fastener at the neck opening on the back.

Beret

For a cute accessory, make a felt beret. Use the pattern on page 65 or draw a circle with a 5½-inch diameter.

Cut two circles from felt. From the center of one circle, cut a smaller, 3-inch-diameter circle, creating a hole to fit the head.

Pin and stitch together the two circles along the outside edge with a running stitch.

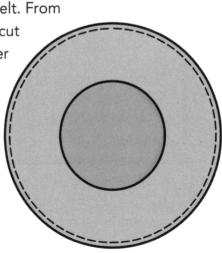

Turn the hat inside out, so the stitched seam is hidden. Pull gently along the opening edge to stretch it a bit. It should fit the doll's head snugly.

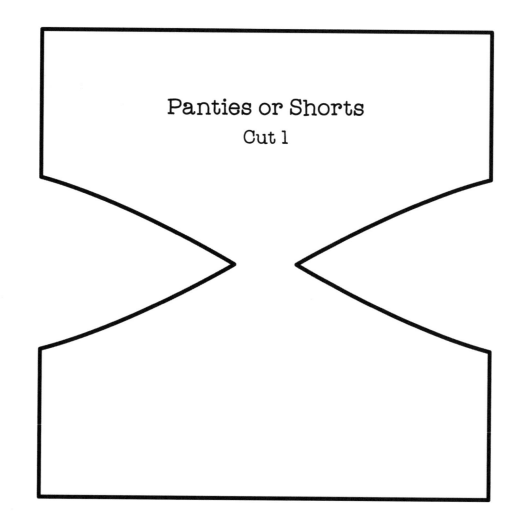

Panties or Shorts

Cut 1

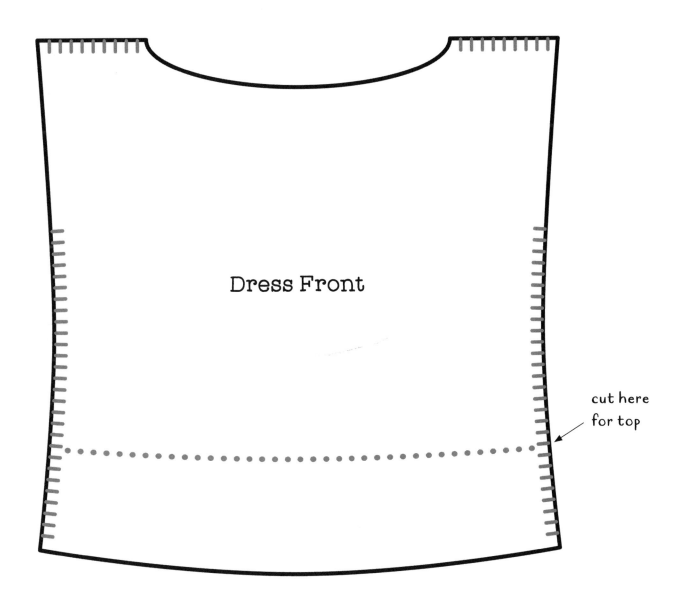

Dress Front

cut here
for top

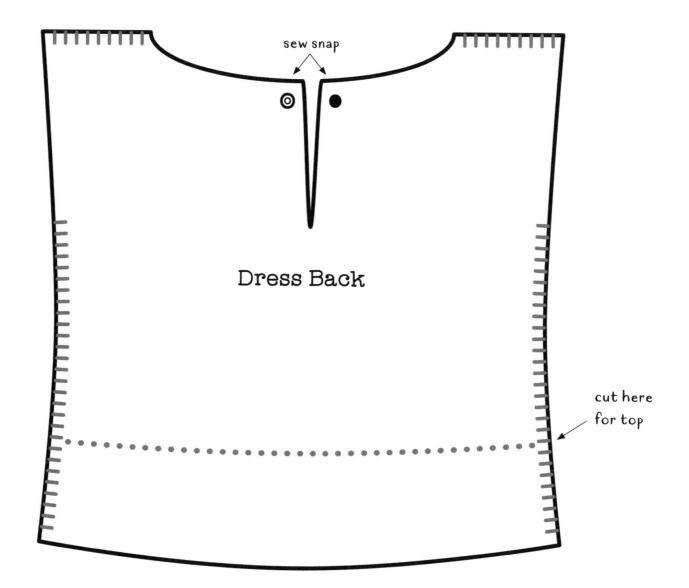

sew snap

Dress Back

cut here
for top

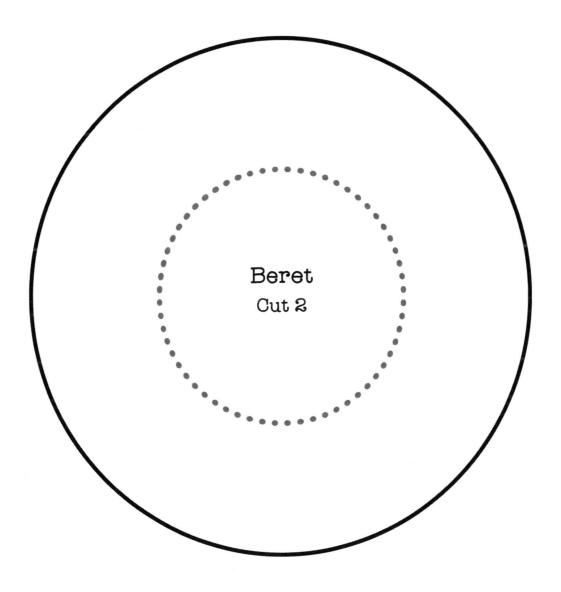

Beret

Cut 2

Fabulous 18-Inch Felt Doll and Outfit

These dolls are lots of fun to dress. Use yarn for their hair and style it with ribbons or sew it in place for ponytails and buns. For short hair, sew craft fur to the head. (See page 6 for instructions for making a craft fur wig.) Because this doll is designed to be made from felt, the sewing is hand stitched on the outside of the doll. Use thread that matches the felt color, making small, even blanket stitches.

MATERIALS

Pencil

Large sheet of paper or newspaper for the pattern

Scissors

Tape

Sewing pins

Felt: flesh color for the doll body and any colors you like for the clothing

Paint brush

Acrylic paints: black, brown or blue, white, light brown, orange, red

Fine-tip markers: black, brown

Needle and thread to match the felt and yarn

Stuffing: polyester or wool

Chopstick or knitting needle

Yarn for hair, about 4 ounces

Hardcover book, about 8 by 10 inches

● Use the pattern pieces shown on pages 67–68 as your guide. You can photocopy the pages, trace the outlines onto thin tracing paper, or draw them on paper with a pencil, adjusting here and there until you are happy with the result.

Cut out the pattern pieces. Tape the leg to the body pattern. Use sewing pins to hold the paper patterns to the felt. Using two pieces of felt, folded in half, cut out two bodies, for front and back. Next, cut out two heads, for front and back.

Draw or paint the face first. It's best to practice on paper or felt scraps. Use a pencil to lightly draw the eyes, nose, and mouth. Paint the entire eye area with white paint, then let dry. Draw or paint the eye color and let dry. Use a black fine-tip marker to outline the

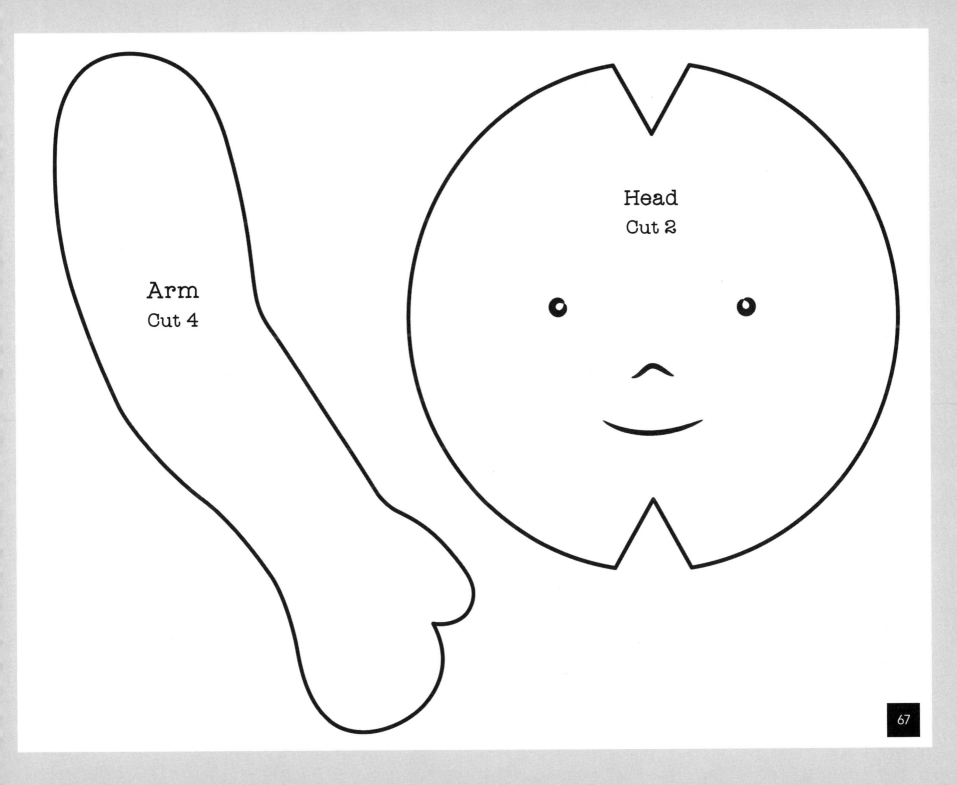

Arm
Cut 4

Head
Cut 2

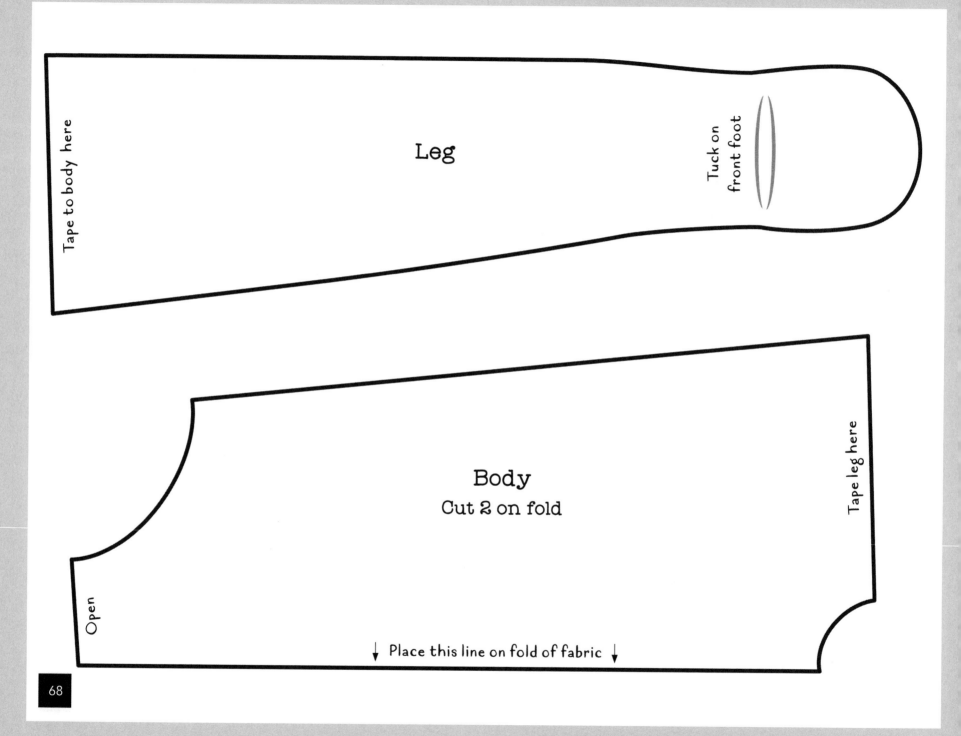

Leg

Tape to body here

Tuck on front foot

Body

Cut 2 on fold

Tape leg here

Open

↓ Place this line on fold of fabric ↓

eye and draw black pupils. With a brown marker, lightly sketch eyebrows and a nose. Draw a thin line for the mouth, then add light lip lines. Fill in the lips with orange, red, and light brown. Bring the features to life with white highlights. Using white paint and the tip of a pencil or a round sewing pin head, make a white dot at the edge of the pupil. Be sure to put the white highlight at the same spot on both eyes. Add a small white dot on the lower lip, on the same side of the head as the eye highlight. It will look like it is reflecting light and will bring the doll's features to life. Let the face dry completely before

handling it again.

Next, sew the body. Pin the two body pieces together, matching the edges. Using a needle and doubled thread, sew along the outer edge of the body with a blanket stitch. Keep your stitches tight and even. Stitch around the legs and torso, leaving the neck

open and openings on both legs. That will allow you to push stuffing into the doll. Lay the body flat and stitch across the top of each leg at the hips, through the body pieces, front to back. Use a running stitch, making small, tight stitches. This will allow the legs to bend at the hip so the doll can sit. Match arm

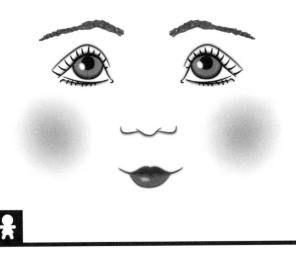

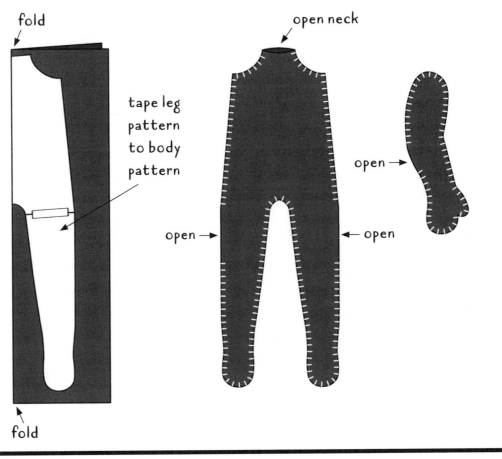

fold

tape leg pattern to body pattern

open neck

open →

← open

open →

fold

pieces together and stitch around the outer edge, leaving an opening about 2 inches wide so you can insert stuffing.

Now you're ready to insert stuffing. Make small wads of stuffing, about the size of Ping-Pong balls. Push stuffing into the hands first, using a chopstick or knitting needle to push stuffing into the smaller areas like the thumbs. When the arm is firmly stuffed, sew the opening closed with blanket stitches. Repeat for the second arm. Push stuffing into both legs and stitch the openings closed. Stuff the body through the neck opening, then stitch the opening closed. On the outside of the finished doll body, turn the feet upward at the front, along

stitch

the ankle. Stitch the top of the foot to the ankle to hold it in place, using tiny hidden stitches.

To create the head and give it a rounder shape, sew the cutout V sections of the head pieces together. Stitch the front and back head

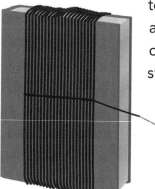

pieces together with a blanket stitch along the outer edges, leaving the neck area open for stuffing. Push stuffing solidly into the head. If the felt wrinkles, you need to add more stuffing. When it's filled, slip the head onto the body neck, turning the edges of the head inside and stitching the head to the neck all around. Use a ladder stitch or a running stitch, sewing through both the head and body. Sew around

the neck twice, so it will be very secure.

Now make the hair. If you are using several colors and types of yarn together, wind the yarns together so they are evenly blended throughout. Wrap the yarn around the longest side of the hardcover book. Continue until the yarn covers the book surface, at least 20 wraps. Using a needle and thread to match the yarn color, begin stitching down the center of the yarn loops using backstitches. Go over your work a second time to be sure all yarns are caught in the stitching.

Turn the yarn-covered book over (stitching side down) and cut through the loops going right down the center. Remove the yarn wig and stitch down any loose yarns on the underside.

Now you're ready to put the wig on the doll's head. Position one end of the stitching at the front of the head, and hold it in place with a sewing pin. Put another sewing pin at the center back, to hold the wig in place. Use running stitches to sew the wig to the head along the stitching line in the wig, going over your work twice to be sure it is attached securely. Now style the hair in ponytails, braids, or buns—even cut bangs if you want. For a thicker, fuller hairstyle, make another yarn wig and sew it on, too.

Chemise or Tank Top

Make a chemise or tank top—or both—from this pattern. They have the same shape, but the tank top stops just below the waist, and the chemise is like a onesie or romper.

MATERIALS

Paper and pencil
Scissors
Felt or other fabric of choice
Sewing pins
Needle and sewing thread
Embroidery thread

Trace or copy the pattern piece onto paper and cut it out. Pin the pattern to felt and cut out two pieces, for front and back. Sew the front and back together at the shoulders, sides, and crotch. With colorful embroidery thread (use three strands), stitch a blanket stitch around the edges of the neck, armholes, and leg holes. That will keep the felt edges from

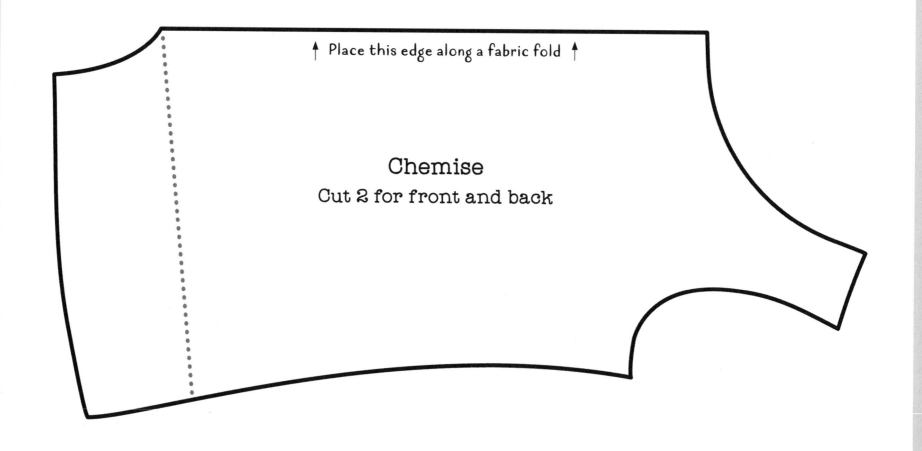

↑ Place this edge along a fabric fold ↑

Chemise

Cut 2 for front and back

stretching out of shape, and it makes a nice trim.

To make a tank top, trim the pattern above the crotch, as shown. Stitch the shoulders and side seams. Decorate it with trim or lace around the neck if you like.

T-Shirt Top or Dress

Old T-shirts make excellent doll clothing because they are thin, stretchy, and, of course, free. If you don't have any stored in your doll maker's stash, you can buy knit fabric at a fabric store, too.

MATERIALS

Measuring tape
T-shirt fabric
Sewing pins
Pen or pencil
Scissors
Needle and matching thread

These drawings are not to scale so can't be used as patterns. Instead, you'll need to take some measurements to ensure a proper fit for your 18-inch doll. Measure across the front of the doll's body. Add 2 inches to that amount. That is how wide the top should be. Measure from the doll's neck to where the lower edge of the shirt will be. If you are making a dress, measure from the neck to where you want the hem to fall. Add ½ inch to that amount, for the shoulder seams.

Prepare the fabric by smoothing it so it lays flat. Pin the back and front of the shirt together so you can cut through both pieces at once, to make a front and back that match in size and shape. Use the hem or the finished edge of the T-shirt as the hem on the project. It saves you time and looks nice.

Use a pen or pencil to lightly mark cutting lines on the T-shirt fabric according to your doll's measurements. Cut along the lines, cutting through both layers of fabric at once.

Turn the pieces "right" side inside and pin them together. Stitch the seams up the sides, leaving arm openings. Try it on the doll to be sure the openings are the right size to fit the arms.

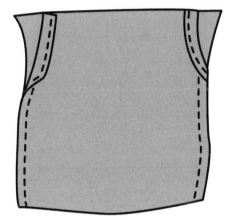

Sew sides. Turn hem inside along the arm opening. Stitch the edge in place.

Turn the armhole edges to the "wrong" side and stitch the edge down to make a slightly curved hem.

Last, sew across the upper edge, making two shoulder seams.

Leave an opening for the doll's neck.

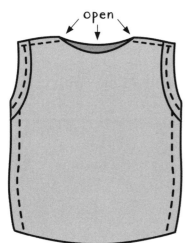

Sew the shoulders together.
Leave an opening for the neck.

Gently stretch the edge of the fab-ric around the neckline so it rolls over itself to create a rolled edging instead of a hem.

Wrap Skirt

This skirt goes nicely with the tank top. Make the top one color and the skirt another, with embroidery thread stitches on the skirt to match the top. Add felt flowers to the skirt, too, to match the top.

MATERIALS

Paper and pencil
Scissors
Felt
Needle and thread
Sew-on snap or button

Use the pattern on page 75 to cut out one back and two front pieces from felt. Sew the back to the fronts at the sides. To keep the edges from stretching at the waist, use three strands of embroidery thread in a blanket stitch all around the edges, from the waist to the hem.

Fit the skirt onto your doll and sew a pair of snaps to fasten the waist. You can use a button, too, with a slit cut for the buttonhole.

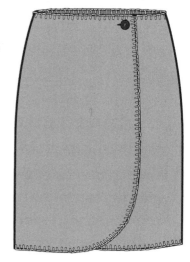

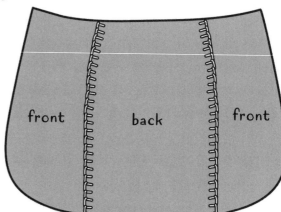

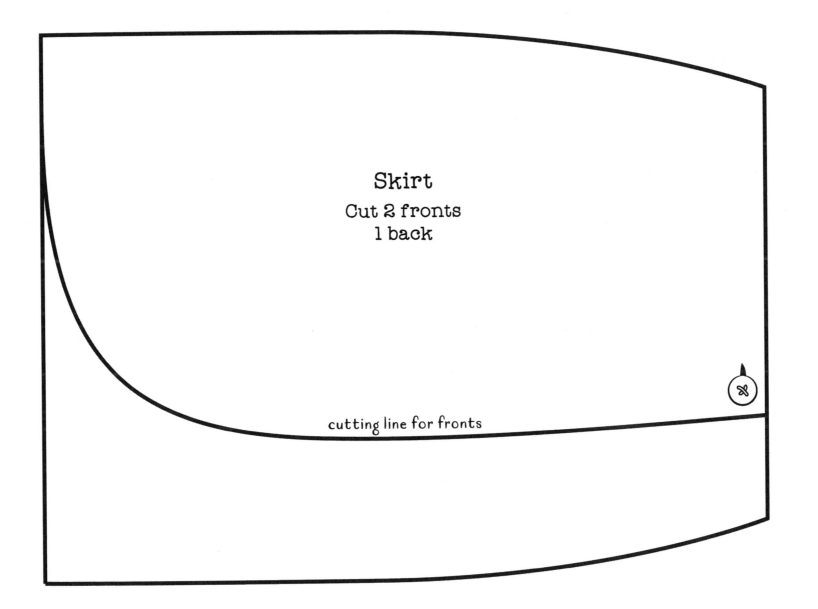

Skirt

Cut 2 fronts
1 back

cutting line for fronts

Painted Cloth Doll

Painted cloth dolls can be simple or elaborate, depending on how much detail you want. You can make a wide range of character dolls: child or adult, beautiful or funny. Look for ideas in advertisements, cartoons, and coloring books. Sketch some designs on scrap paper before working on the fabric. Keep the outline simple so the sewing part is easy, then make more difficult dolls as you gain skills.

MATERIALS

Newspapers to cover work surface
Muslin or other lightweight woven fabric
Pencil
Cup of water and paper towels
Paintbrush
Acrylic paints
Fine-tip permanent markers: black and brown
Scissors
Sewing pins
Needle and thread
Stuffing: polyester or wool
Felt squares in several colors
Light cardboard (optional)
Yarn, fake fur, felt strips, or fringe (optional)

◉ Start with a simple doll made by drawing directly on muslin with permanent markers. Add details with colored pencils, pens, or crayons.

Move on to painted dolls, working as if you are making a watercolor painting. Cover the work area with old newspapers before starting, to protect from paint stains. You can outline the figure on muslin with pencil first, then wet the entire piece of fabric a bit with a brush and water. Paint in areas with different colors, letting them slightly blend together while wet. Let the piece dry completely, then draw over the painted areas with fine-tip permanent markers to create the details.

Once your design is completely dry, trim it away from the background fabric, leaving about ½ inch all around the design for a seam.

Lay that doll image piece on another layer of muslin, and cut another piece the same size for the doll's back. Turn those two pieces so the image's "right" side is on the inside and pin the pieces together to hold them in place. Stitch around the outside edge with running stitches or back-stitches. Leave an opening near the base of the doll large enough to fit your hand. Clip away the excess seam fabric at any curves or corners so the doll will lie flat once it's turned right side out.

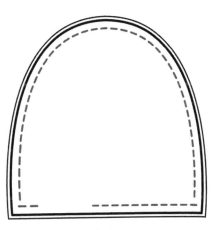

Now turn the doll right side out and stuff until it is as solid as you want. Then stitch the opening closed. Be sure to tuck the raw edges of the fabric along the opening to the inside as you stitch.

If you want a stuffed doll that stands on its own, make an oval from fabric and another from light cardboard to make it hold its shape. Sew the back and front of the doll together, leaving the bottom edges open. Sew the edge of the fabric oval to the bottom of the doll, halfway around. Turn the doll right-side out. Slide the cardboard in place inside the doll, then finish stitching around the rest of the oval, leaving an opening to insert stuffing. Stitch the opening closed.

If you want a more challenging project, make arms that are sewn

stuff, then sew closed

and stuffed, then pinned in place on the doll's body front before stitching the outer seam. Feet can be sewn, stuffed, and stitched the same way, adding them before sewing the outside seam.

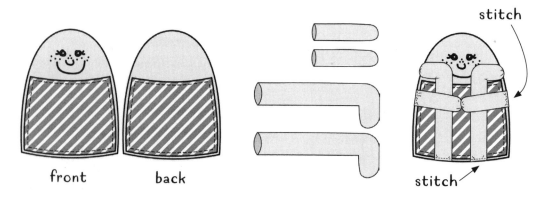

front   back   stitch

stitch

Position the two body pieces together so the "right" side is inside and pin around the edges. Stitch the outer edges of the doll together all around, leaving an opening so you can turn the doll right side out. Stuff the doll by pushing wads of stuffing through the opening, then stitch it closed with tiny stitches.

If you want to add hair, sew or glue on yarn, fake fur, felt strips, or fringe. Or draw hair with a marker or paint.

leave opening

Bendy Doll

While this appears to be a simple doll, its design is actually more complex than that of the soft dolls. Bendy dolls have an armature, or skeleton, inside that is flexible and can be moved and posed. You'll use pipe cleaners for this project, but if you want to make more complicated and realistic dolls, you can use wire, covering it with stuffing or padding, then a body fabric.

Get started with these little pipe cleaner bendies. They are fun to bend into action poses and are quick to make, too. Save scraps and bits of materials to make their clothing and accessories. There are two ways to make them. Choose the felt body for a quick elf-type doll (see page 82), or these yarn-wrapped dolls for a bit more detail.

MATERIALS

2 12-inch-long pipe cleaners
Yarn
Scissors
Yarn needle (optional)
Craft glue
Round wood bead (25 millimeters, about 1 inch diameter)
Scraps of felt and cloth (optional)
Needle and thread (optional)
Fine-tip markers or acrylic paint and a toothpick (optional)

◉ Bend and fold one pipe cleaner in half. That will be the body. Twist the ends of the other pipe cleaner together to form a loop.

Flatten the loop and slide it inside the first pipe cleaner. It will become the arms. Position it about 1 inch from the fold, which will be the neck. Twist the body pipe cleaner above and below the arm section to hold it in place. Bend the ends of the body piece back about ½ inch to form feet.

Wrap the pipe cleaner skeleton with colorful yarn. Make it as fat or skinny as you want. Use one yarn color for the entire body if you like, or use one for the shirt and a different color for the pants. If you are going to make a dress for a girl doll, wrap the skeleton with a color that will be the body, because later you will make a dress to go over it. Use a fun color or black for the legs so it looks like tights to go with the dress.

Begin wrapping around the chest area first, to give the doll shape. Crisscross over the chest and around the neck and arms, then wrap tightly to the wrists and back up the arms, leaving the hands uncovered. Hide the end of the yarn under the next color.

Wrap the pants or tights, leaving the feet uncovered. When you are finished, clip the working end of the yarn about 8 inches long. Thread it onto a yarn needle and slip it into the body twice to secure it, then clip the end and hide it inside the yarn wraps.

Put a drop of glue on the neck end and slip the wooden bead onto it.

To make a dress for your bendy doll, use the pattern here to cut one piece from cloth. Fold it at the neck, with the "right" side inside, and sew the sides together. With scissors, clip the fabric to the stitching under the arms, so it won't bunch up under the doll's arms. Turn the dress right side out and slip it onto the doll's body feetfirst.

fold here

Dress

clip inner corner

Make a yarn wig for a long-haired doll by wrapping yarn around your hand 15 times. Slip the loops off your hand, keeping them together. Use a short piece of matching yarn to tie and knot the loops together. Cut the opposite end of the loops. Apply craft glue to the top of the bead head, press the wig onto the head, hold until it's sticky, and let dry.

Make a simple felt hat by cutting a circle for a brim, then cut out the center circle to fit the bead head. Cut another circle, a bit smaller than the brim circle.

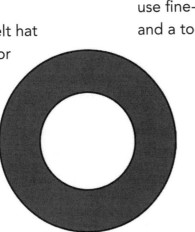

Cut out a pie slice–shaped section of the circle so it won't be so bulky. Apply glue to the bead head and wrap and press the hat onto the head. Apply a line of glue around the edge of the hat and slip the brim onto it. Press the pieces together until they hold.

Add a face if you want—just use fine-tip markers or acrylic paint and a toothpick.

Action Figures

Little painted plastic dolls called action figures were introduced in 1964. They were marketed to boys and not called dolls (even though they were) because marketers thought boys wouldn't buy them if they thought dolls were just for girls. The figures were soldiers, wrestlers, and superheroes that flexed arms and legs and could hold poses. They didn't have a wardrobe, as dolls marketed to girls did, but action figures did come with lots of accessories such as guns and helmets, as well as vehicles they could ride in.

Elf Doll

Elves are fantasy creatures that people have been talking about for centuries. They are said to live underground and usually described as helpful, harmless little beings. They are fun to have around, so make one or many. Since no one has actually seen one, they can all look a bit different.

MATERIALS

2 12-inch-long pipe cleaners
Paper and pencil
Scissors
Felt
Craft glue
Needle and thread (optional)
Round wood bead (25 millimeter, about 1 inch diameter)
Wool roving, thick yarn, or cotton ball (optional)
Fine-tip permanent marker or acrylic paint and toothpick

⬤ Follow the directions for the bendy doll skeleton (see page 79), but don't wrap it with yarn. Use the patterns on page 83 to cut out one suit and one hat from felt. Fold the suit at the shoulders and slip it onto the doll, over the feet first. Apply craft glue to the pipe cleaner body and press the suit down onto it. You can also stitch the suit together. Slip the suit onto the body and stitch all around the outside edges with blanket stitch.

Fold the cap in half lengthwise, and stitch the back seam.

Squirt some glue onto the bead head and slip the cap into place, putting the seam in the back so it doesn't show. If you want your elf to have a beard, glue wool roving, thick yarn, or a cotton ball in place. If you want to add a face, draw it with a permanent fine-tip marker or acrylic paint and a toothpick.

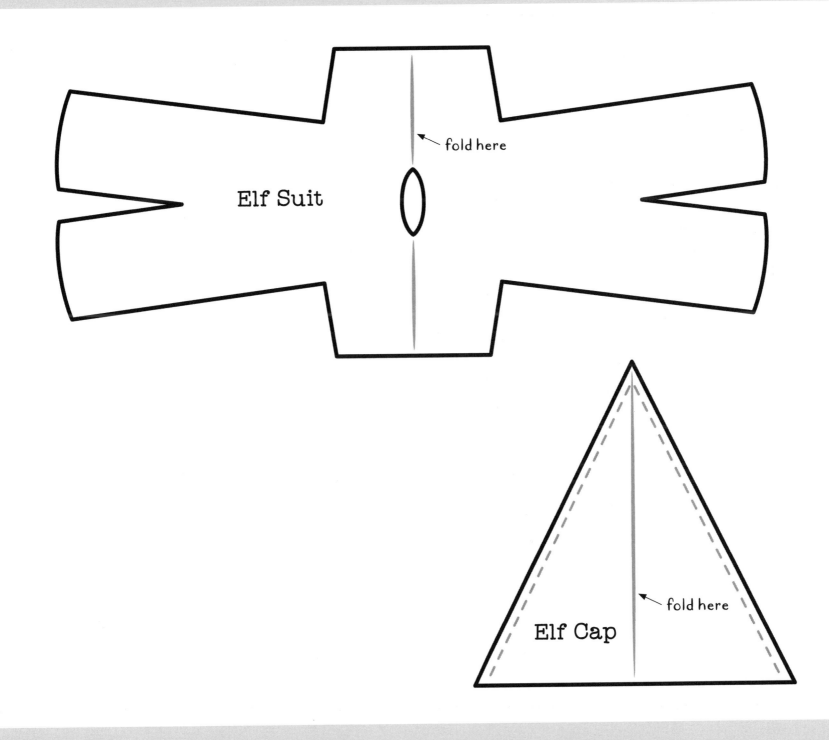

Elf Suit

fold here

Elf Cap

fold here

Recycled and Renewed Doll

You can change the look of a plastic doll by repainting the face. You can recycle and repurpose discarded dolls or dolls from thrift shops. With fresh faces and cleaned-up hair, they are practically new again. If you want to see how stunning such changes can be, check out Sonia Singh's "Tree Change Dolls" at www.treechangedolls.com.au.

ADULT SUPERVISION REQUIRED

MATERIALS

Plastic doll (Do NOT use an expensive doll, such as an American Girl doll, unless you have a parent's or guardian's permission. With this project there is no going back, and the doll will never look like it did in the beginning. For recycled dolls, that's the whole reason for doing this project. But for expensive or collectible dolls, it can destroy their value, so ask first.)

Soap

Washcloth

Shampoo

Towel

Comb

Scissors

Rubber band

Plastic wrap

Tape

Nail polish remover or acetone

Paper towels or tissues

Watercolor pencils (dark brown, blue, green, black, pink, red, orange)

Small paintbrushes: one pointed and one flat

Acrylic paint (white)

Chalk pastels (pink, orange, red) or makeup blusher

Spray acrylic sealer (matte finish, not shiny gloss finish)

To start, you'll want to wash the doll. Use a basin of warm soapy water and a soft washcloth. Scrub the doll's body and face, removing stains and scuffs. Wash the hair with warm water and shampoo. Dry with a towel, then comb the hair to untangle it. Trim the ends if they are rough and uneven. Let the hair dry completely before working on the face. Pull the hair out of the way with a rubber band, so no paint will get on it. Wrap the doll's body and hair with plastic food wrap, holding it in place with some tape. That will protect the doll from paint and the sealer finishing spray.

Use nail polish remover and scraps of paper towel to scrub away the paint on the doll's face. Dolls vary, so it might be easy or take several minutes of scrubbing to get all the paint off. The doll will dry very quickly, so as soon as the paint is removed completely, you are ready to begin the new face.

Work on the face from the top down, so you don't accidentally smear with your hands as you work. Alternate working on the eyes as you do each step, so they are alike.

Use sharp watercolor pencils to draw the eyes first. With dark brown, outline the eyelids and darken the edge of the upper lid so it is darker and thicker than the lower lid. Draw a circle in the center, which will be the pupil. Still using dark brown, draw outlines for the iris (colored

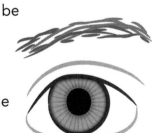

part) and fill it in with the eye color you choose—blue, green, brown—using a watercolor pencil. Use white pencil to fill in the white parts of the eyeball. Darken the pupil with a black pencil.

Add tiny brown lashes with a sharp pencil along both the top and bottom eyelids. Draw the lashes so they curve away from the center of the eye. Make the upper lashes longer and thicker than the lower lashes.

Check that both eyes are the same and make any changes you need now. If you don't like something, just wipe it with a wet cloth to remove and start over.

Use a sharp brown pencil to draw lightly into both nostrils, just to give a shadow inside the nose. Sketch light eyebrows, too. Continue with the brown pencil, and draw a line between the lips, which will give a shadow to the mouth.

Add color to the lips, making the upper lip a bit darker than the lower lip. Use pink, red, and orange pencils, blending the colors to get just the right look.

Now add some white highlights to make the face look more lifelike. With a fine-tip pointed paintbrush (or toothpick) and white acrylic paint, make a dot on the edge of both eye pupils. Make sure the dots are on the same side of both

eyes and are the same size. Isn't it surprising how they sparkle now?

Add a highlight to the lower lip, too, making a small dash on the center lower lip, on the same side of the face as the eye highlights.

Let the paint dry completely. Then add some blush to the doll's face with a stiff flat paintbrush. Dust pink, orange, or red dry chalk pastels or makeup blusher onto the cheeks and a bit on the tip of the nose and center of the forehead. It will add more life to the doll's face.

Take the doll outdoors or to a well-ventilated space and have an adult help you spray a thin coat

of acrylic sealer (matte finish, so it isn't glossy) on the face. Don't use too much or it will create drips. Just lightly spray some puffs to seal in the pencil and chalk. Let the doll dry completely before handling it.

Doll Hospitals

Workshops that repair dolls first appeared about 300 years ago and are found around the world. They are called doll hospitals, and there is even a Doll Doctor's Association in the United States. Most customers are adults who want a childhood favorite restored or collectors who want to repair a valuable doll.

Doll Clothes and Accessories

If you have gathered lots of fabric, trims, and fasteners for your doll maker's toolkit, you'll have plenty of options for your clothing projects. Also, look for scraps or pieces of thin plastic (for shoes and handbags), fake fur (for coat collars), jewelry pieces, leather, and anything else that might be useful. Fabric should not be stiff or difficult to work with, as heavy denim can be. And as a reminder, fabrics with large prints look out of proportion to a doll. Small-scale prints look better.

Felt is perfect for making doll clothing because it is so easy to use. It has no "right" or "wrong" side—it's the same on both sides. The edges won't fray or unravel like woven or knitted cloth because it's made by pressing the fibers flat. That means you don't have to worry about turning and sewing hems on felt clothes. You can use stitches or even glue to hold pieces of felt together. Felt clothing doesn't slip off a doll easily, either, like silky fabrics do. It comes in lots of colors and is sold in packages so you can have a variety of colors to choose from without buying yards of fabric.

If you choose felt made from recycled plastic bottles (Eco-fi is one brand) you are helping the environment and creating something clever from discarded bottles. Plastic bottles are cut up, melted, and squirted into threads that are pressed into polyester craft felt. Twelve bottles can make one pound or two yards of the felt.

Wool felt, made from sheep's fleece, is natural and has been made for centuries. It's warm and lasts forever. It's expensive and hard to find in most fabric stores; however, you can buy it online or have a store order it for you.

Whatever felt you use, save every scrap because even small pieces can make little flowers or decorations for lots of garments. You can chop up the felt into small pieces and use them for stuffing, too.

Collect other materials for your projects, too. Save them in boxes or use an old suitcase that can be stored under your bed.

Fashion Dolls Before Magazines

Dolls have an interesting role in spreading fashion and clothing trends. Long ago, before magazines and television spread photographs and images of popular new clothing styles, dolls were dressed and sent out to show people what was new. Wealthy people had the clothing copied by dressmakers. People could look at the doll's attire and order the clothing in their size. Peddlers would carry dolls to show items that could be ordered. Around 1850, one group of women actually wore their newly ordered wool capes on their heads as scarves until the dolls arrived and showed them the garments were meant to be fastened at the neck.

Discarded clothing has loads of potential uses. Wash the clothing first. Then cut off and save buttons, lace trims, shoelaces—even zippers. Lay the clothing flat and trim off the waistband, sleeves, or pockets—any areas you won't be able to use. Cut the clothing apart at the seams so you can fold it to store flat.

Wash and dry old wool or cashmere sweaters at hot temperatures so the fabric will shrink and "felt." Use for clothing or cut into strips and sew or glue on a doll for hair.

Measuring and Making It Fit

A measuring tape is an important tool when you are designing and sewing clothing for dolls (or yourself). It's a waste of time and fabric to just guess what size or shape something should be, when you can be accurate and successful by measuring first. Woodworkers have a saying: "Measure twice, cut once." Lumber cannot be glued back together if cut wrong. For designers, it's best to "Measure once, write it down, then cut."

Make a Doll Dress Form

Want to try your hand at designing clothing for your doll? Work like the pros do, and use a dress form. Make a few extra mannequins (a French word for dress form) so you can display your doll's clothing, too. This project is designed for an 18-inch doll.

ADULT SUPERVISION REQUIRED

MATERIALS

Plastic doll

Plastic food wrap

Duct tape: If you choose a tape with a pattern printed on it, instead of plain gray, wrinkles won't show up as much in the finished form—and it looks a lot nicer in a pretty design.

Scissors

Candleholder (from a dollar store or resale shop)

Wood dowel to fit the holder (usually a ¾-inch dowel, about 12 inches long)

Spray paint, acrylic paint, or latex paint

Wood glue or hot glue gun

Plastic grocery bags (about 20)

⬤ Use an undressed doll for the form. Wrap it tightly in a couple layers of plastic wrap. Be sure to wrap over the shoulders and across the back and front at the neck. Wrap around the arms, but don't cover the arms. Wrap across the bottom at the hips. The wrap will keep the tape and any adhesive from sticking to the doll. If you forget this step it will be very difficult to get all the tape off the doll.

Tear or cut duct tape into short pieces, about 4 inches long, and begin wrapping the doll, covering the plastic wrap. Cover the entire torso with at least three layers of tape. You want it to be firm once it's off the doll, so the more tape, the less likely it will get dented and out of shape. Press firmly after applying each piece of tape, to smooth out any wrinkles.

When the doll's torso is covered with layers of tape, use the tip of the scissors to begin snipping through the layers of tape and plastic wrap in the back. Cut from the bottom up to the neck, being careful not to nick the doll.

Slip the form off the doll and carefully tape the back together. Add more tape strips to cover the arm and neck openings. Trim the bottom edge with scissors so it is even all the way around.

You can attach the form to a base made from a candleholder and dowel. Paint them first, using acrylic, latex, or spray paint (with an adult's help), and let dry completely. Then glue the dowel section into the candleholder, using wood glue or hot glue.

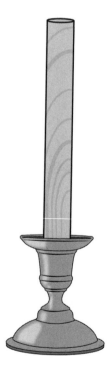

Begin stuffing the inside of the dress form with plastic grocery bags. Fill the form and make it solid so it will hold its shape. Slip the dowel into the bottom of the dress form and push it gently up to the neck area, stuffing bags in to hold it in place. Tape across the base to hold in the bags and completely cover the bottom. Adjust the dowel for height and finish taping everything securely.

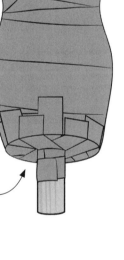

Stuff the form. Insert dowel. Adjust for height, then tape the base, securing the dowel.

No-Sew Ballerina Skirt

This skirt is fun to make and wear. Once you make one for your doll, you can use the same instructions and materials to make a larger one for yourself.

MATERIALS

Nylon netting or other thin, silky fabric

Ribbon: about ½ inch wide and 30 inches long

Scissors

● Cut strips of netting fabric about ½ inch wide and twice as long as you want the skirt to be. Double each strip and fold the loop over the ribbon, pulling the ends of the fabric strip through the loop. You'll be making a lark's head knot. The ribbon will become a waistband. Keep tying strips onto the waistband until the skirt is large enough to wrap around your doll.

Wrap and tie the ends of the ribbon in a bow.

No-Sew T-Shirt Dress

No time to sew? Here's how you can create a superquick and easy new dress when your doll needs one. Use new knit fabric or a discarded T-shirt.

MATERIALS

T-shirt (or knit fabric)
Scissors
Measuring tape
String or yarn, about 18 inches
Pencil
Ribbon or yarn tie for a belt

⬤ Cut the sleeves off the T-shirt and cut up one side along the underarm. Open the fabric and smooth it flat. You will be working with a single layer of fabric. Decide how long you want the dress to be on the doll. Measure the doll with the measuring tape from the neckline to where you want the hemline to be. That is measurement A.

Tie the end of a piece of string around the pencil. Measure and cut the string the same length as A. Hold the cut end of the string down with your thumb (or have a friend help) in the center of the fabric. Pull the string till it's tight, then draw with the pencil all around to make a circle. (For an 18-inch doll, your circle should be 20 inches across.)

Cut out the circle. Make a neck hole in the center by folding the circle in half, then in half again. Cut across the point, cutting away a small amount of fabric. Cut away enough so that the hole will fit over your doll's head.

20"

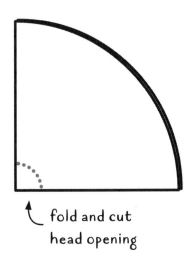

fold and cut
head opening

Now unfold the fabric one time so the circle is folded in half, and cut two armholes along the fold, on either side of the neck hole, as shown.

Slip the dress onto the doll and tie a ribbon or yarn piece around the waist for a belt.

No-Sew Tube Sock Top and Skirt

This outfit will fit an 18-inch doll if you use adult-sized socks. Use smaller socks for smaller dolls. Since socks stretch, they can fit a variety of doll sizes. You can make this top and skirt from matching socks, or choose different color socks for each.

MATERIALS

2 socks (tube-style sport socks are best)

Scissors

Top

Lay the doll flat on the table and lay the sock on top, to figure out how long to make the top. Then lay the sock flat on the table. The ribbed sock opening will be the roll-down neckline. Cut straight across the sock, at the place where you want the bottom hemline to be.

← cut

Cut two holes for the arms to pass through. Gently pull across the lower edge to stretch the fabric until it rolls up, making a rolled edging that doesn't need a hem.

Skirt

Repeat the steps for the top with another sock, using the ribbed cuff edge as the waistband on the skirt, except don't cut out armholes. Gently stretch the hemline so it rolls upward, too.

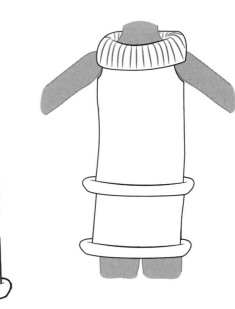

Poncho

This is an easy top to make and fit on a doll because there are no sleeves or waistline. It's a nice boho (Bohemian) look from the 1970s, which is very popular now.

MATERIALS

Measuring tape
Paper and pencil
Fabric: felt is best, but you can
   use almost any woven fabric
Scissors
Needle and thread
Trim: lace, fringe, embroidery
   thread (optional)

⬤ Measure from the doll's neck to the middle of its arm. That is measurement A. Measure from the doll's center torso (belly button location) to the doll's center back, going over the shoulder with the measuring tape. That is measurement B.

Measure and mark two rectangles on the fabric. Use measurement A for the width and measurement B for the length. Cut them out.

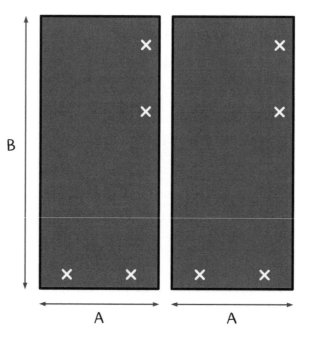

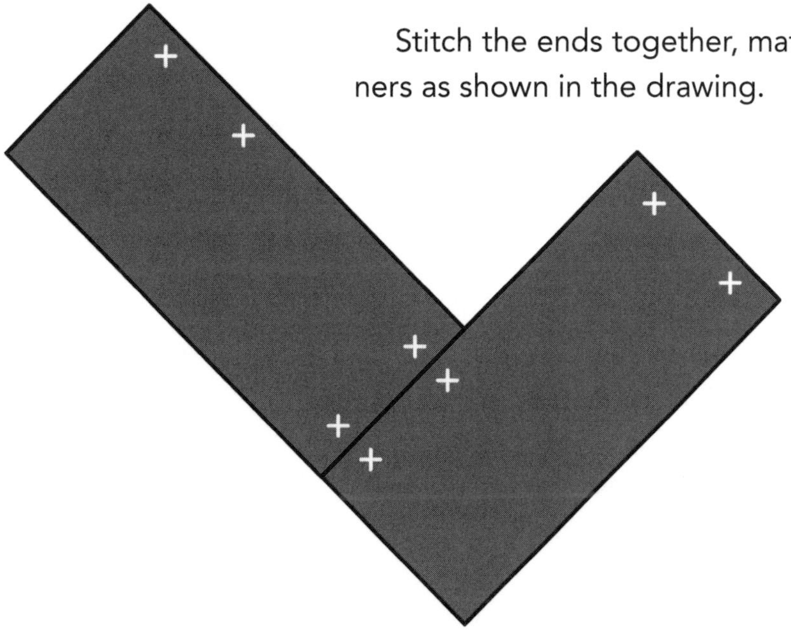

Stitch the ends together, matching up corners as shown in the drawing.

If you want to add a strip of fringe or lace to the edge, stitch it in place. If using felt, there's no need to hem the poncho, but you might want to trim it with decorative stitching, such as a blanket stitch around the edges with bright colored embroidery thread. Or glue on felt flowers, fish, or other shapes.

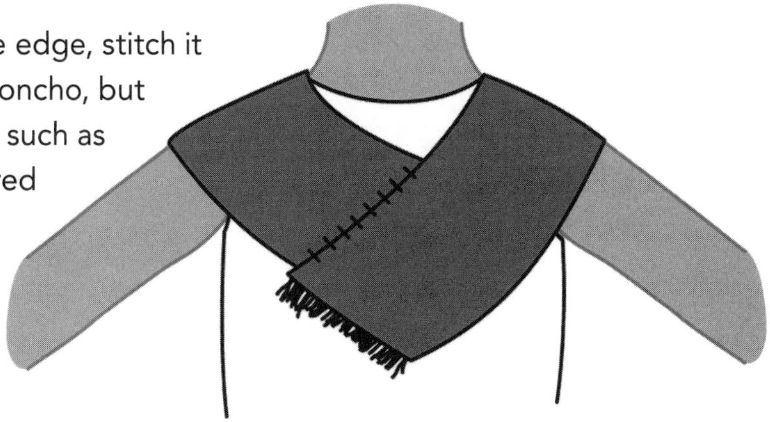

Basic Dress or Top

This is a very basic garment that can be used as a dress, long gown, crop top, shirt, or coat—it's very versatile. Just change the length, sleeves, and trim. Make an entire wardrobe to fit any doll.

MATERIALS

Measuring tape

Pen

Newspaper

Scissors

Felt: enough to make the front and back for a garment to fit your doll

Sewing pins

Needle and matching thread

Sew-on snap fastener, button, ribbon, or yarn

⦾ Decide whether to make a dress, long gown, or top. Do you want long sleeves or short? Just by changing the pattern piece, you can make lots of different looks.

Measure the doll from its neck to where you want the bottom of the garment to end. That is measurement A. Measure from one wrist across the arms and chest to the other wrist. That is measurement B. If you want shorter sleeves, measure from the edge of one sleeve across the doll's body to the other edge of the sleeve.

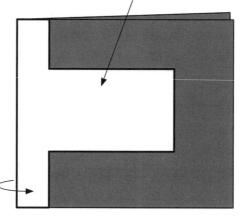

paper pattern

fold

Draw a pattern on newspaper using those measurements, making A the length and B the width. Use the measuring tape to determine how wide to make the sleeves. Draw the outline, then cut out the pattern. Fold the felt piece so you can place the shoulder edge of the pattern along the fold. That way you won't have shoulder seams. Place the pattern on the felt, pinning it to secure it while you cut it out around the edges.

Fold the cutout dress in half lengthwise, then in half crosswise. Clip out a small circle at the center of the folded point. Open the felt and you'll see that you have created the neck hole. Adjust the size as needed to fit your doll's neck size. Cut a slit down the center of the dress back to make an opening so the dress can be put on the doll easily.

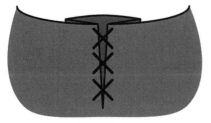

To make the neckline fit better, make a pleat at the center front neck by folding to make two tucks as shown. Stitch across to hold the pleat in place.

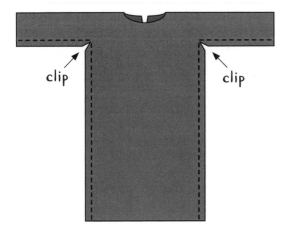

clip   clip

Stitch the side seams, turning the corner under the arm, and ending at the edge of the sleeve. With the tip of the scissors, cut a tiny clip in the corner fabric. Be careful to NOT cut the stitching. This will give room under the arm so it won't bunch up.

Turn the garment seam-side to the inside and sew a snap or button at the neck. You can use two pieces of ribbon or yarn ties to fasten the back neck in a bow if you want. Add any trim you like.

With a few changes you can make the pattern as a simple top or as a button-front coat. Make a top by making shorter sleeves and stopping the length at the waist.

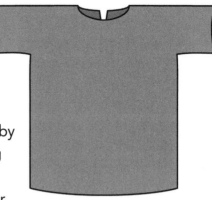

Make a button-up shirt or jacket by cutting the front open and adding pockets and buttons. Sew two rectangle pieces to the neck for a collar.

Button Up!

Do you know which side of a garment opening buttons should be placed on? For girls' clothing, buttons go on the left side of the garment. For guys' clothing, buttons are sewn on the right side. This practice goes back to the time when wealthy women were dressed by their maids, and buttons on the left side of the garment were easier for right-handed maids to work with. Men were left to do their own buttons, it seems.

Camisole and Undies

*T*his project can also be used to make a tank top or T-shirt. Use a large sock to make this fit an 18-inch doll.

MATERIALS

Sock with a ribbed cuff
Scissors
Needle
Embroidery thread

Camisole

Cut away the toe of the sock, then cut off the ribbed cuff. Lay the center sock section flat on the table and cut out arm and neck areas. Try it on the doll and adjust to fit, cutting larger holes if needed. Fold or roll the cut edges inward around the neck and armholes, to the inside of the shirt, and stitch a hem. Use embroidery thread and a blanket stitch. You can use matching color thread if you want, but it also looks nice with a colorful thread stitched around the neck and armholes. Add a stitched flower embroidered at the front neck, too.

Gently pull and stretch the lower edge of the shirt, so it rolls up at the bottom. That makes a nice rolled finish and won't unravel.

Undies

Use the remaining sock cuff section from the camisole project. The finished edge of the sock will be the undies waistband. Use the doll as a guide and cut the center of the cuff through both layers to make legs. Turn the cuff "right" side in, and fold the cut edge down about ¼ inch. Stitch a hem around the edge with three strands of colored embroidery thread using a blanket stitch. Lay the undies flat and locate the center. Sew three or four stitches at the center to create a crotch. That's it! Just turn right side out and slip the undies onto the doll.

Felt Short Shorts

These shorts can also be used as panties or a swimsuit bottom.

MATERIALS

Measuring tape
Felt or fabric
Scissors
Needle and thread to match felt
Colorful embroidery thread

● Measure across the doll's hips from side to side. Add 1 inch for seams. That will be measurement A. Measure down the doll's side from its waist to where you want the bottom edge of the shorts, which will be measurement B.

Lay out the felt or fabric and fold it in half. Measure A across the fold, and B down from the fold. Cut out the rectangle along those measurements, cutting through both layers of felt but not cutting through the center fold. Make two diagonal cuts along the sides of the fold to create leg openings. The fold will be the crotch.

Stitch seams up both sides, using matching thread and a blanket stitch. Try the panties on the doll, to be sure the leg openings are cut large enough. Adjust as needed.

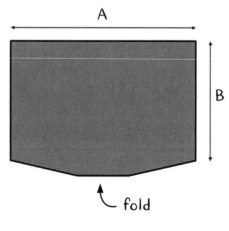

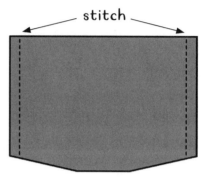

Stitch a blanket stitch using three strands of colorful embroidery thread around the openings at the waist and legs. It will be a cute trim and will keep the felt from stretching out of shape when you dress the doll.

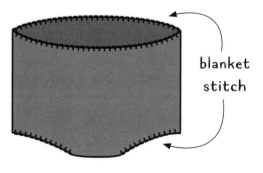

Summer Dress or Top

This dress takes some sewing but will fit most any doll shape because it adjusts with ribbon ties at the shoulders.

MATERIALS

Measuring tape
Fabric
Scissors
Thin ribbon or yarn for shoulder
    ties
Small safety pin
Needle and matching thread
Lace, rickrack, or other trim
    (optional)

⬤ Lay the doll on a table and measure across the torso from side to side. Double that number. That is measurement A. Measure from the doll's neck to the bottom length you want to garment to be. Add 2 inches to that number for measurement B.

Cut two fabric rectangles as wide as A and as long as B. Fold 1 inch down across the top edge of both rectangles. Stitch to create a casing, or tunnel, for the ribbon to slide through. Sew the two rectangles together along the sides, leaving openings at the top on both sides for armholes.

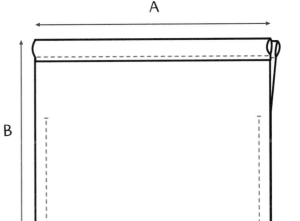

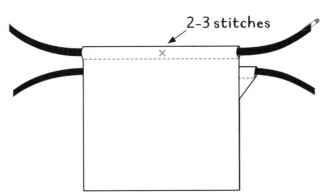

2-3 stitches

Cut two pieces of ribbon each twice as long as A. Fasten a small safety pin to one end of the ribbon and use it to push the ribbon through the casing. Then remove the pin and repeat the process with the other piece of ribbon going through the other casing. Extend the ribbons evenly from both sides of the garment. With a needle and thread, stitch two or three stitches through the center of the ribbon and garment, to hold the ribbon and keep it from pulling out of the casing. Do this on both the front and back of the shirt or dress.

Tie the ribbons at the shoulders and adjust the gathered fabric till it looks nice.

Fold up the bottom of the garment and stitch a hem if you want; or trim the bottom with lace, rickrack, or other trim.

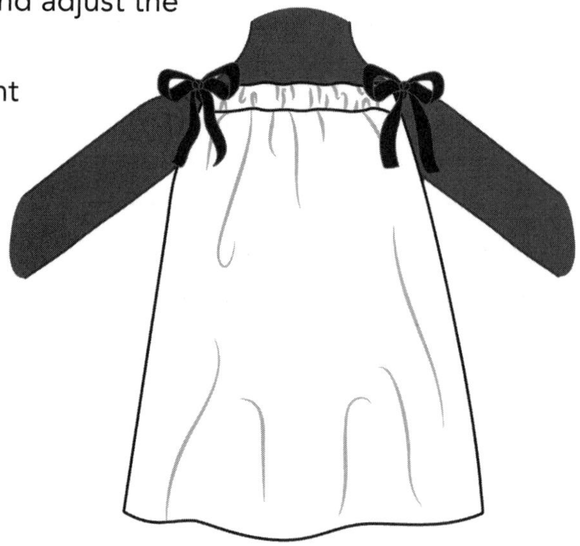

Pants or Shorts

Make these bottoms any length you like—ankle pants, capris, or shorts. To create leggings for your doll, make them long and slim-fitting.

MATERIALS

Measuring tape
Fabric that stretches (T-shirt or other jersey knit)
Scissors
Sewing pins
Pencil or fabric marking pen
Needle and thread

● Measure across the doll's hips and add 1 inch to each side (measurement A). Measure the doll from the waist to the shoe top and add 1½ inches (measurement B). Lay the fabric flat and cut two rectangles that are A across and B in length. Measure from the doll's waist to the center of the crotch; add 2 inches. Lay the rectangles on top of each other, pinned together so they don't move as you cut. Mark the crotch point. Draw leg lines from the bottom edge to the crotch point and cut out the center of the pants on those lines.

Pin the pants pieces together with the "right" side inside. Sew the side seams, then sew the center crotch seam. Clip through the seam fabric at the point of the crotch seam, being careful not to clip through the stitching. It will turn and lie flat easier. Turn the waist edge down 1 inch and stitch it in place. Turn the pant legs up ½ inch and sew a hem.

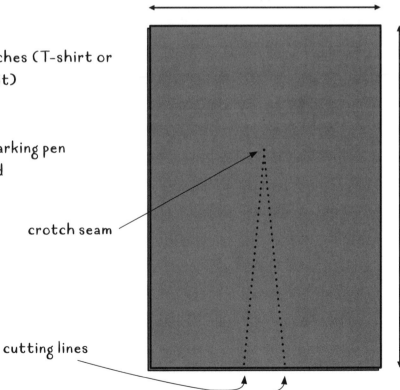

crotch seam

cutting lines

A

B

Turn the pants right side out and slip onto the doll. If they are baggy at the back waist, sew a couple of tucks so the pants fit better but are still loose enough to pull on and off.

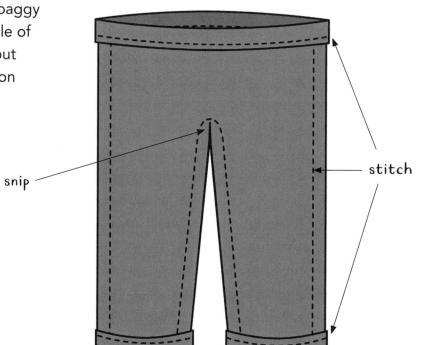

snip

stitch

Felt Sundress and Jacket

This outfit can have many options. The dress can be made as a jumper or apron. The jacket can be made longer as a bathrobe. Make it even longer and add buttons to make a coat. It will fit an 18-inch doll.

MATERIALS

Measuring tape
Scissors
Felt
Paper and pencil
Needle and embroidery thread
Sewing pins
Buttons or snaps

Dress

Measure and cut one skirt piece 7 by 14 inches. Set it aside.

To make the dress top front, cut a 3 by 5-inch rectangle. Fold the rectangle in half widthwise and trim the top corner (not the folded edge) on a curve.

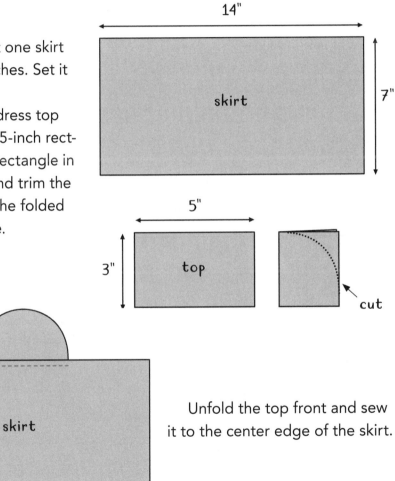

Unfold the top front and sew it to the center edge of the skirt.

Cut two straps, each 7 inches long and 2 inches wide. Fold each strap in half and stitch around the outer edge with a blanket stitch.

Sew the skirt together at the back seam. Try it on your doll and pin the straps in place. Sew the straps to the back of the skirt with the ends hidden inside the skirt.

back view   front view

Adjust the straps to fit. Sew a button on the front of each strap and cut tiny slits in the dress front for buttonholes, or sew snaps to the front and to the straps.

Jacket

Cut a 9 by 12-inch felt rectangle. Fold it in half widthwise. Pin the edges to hold the fabric as you work. To create sleeves, cut away rectangles that are 2 inches wide and 1 inch tall from the bottom side corners of the front and back.

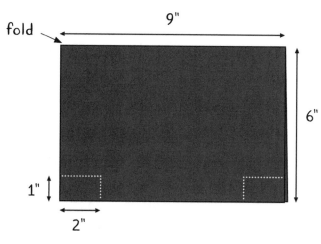

Now fold the piece in half again to find the neck center. Trim away that corner to make a neck opening. You may have to cut it large to fit the doll.

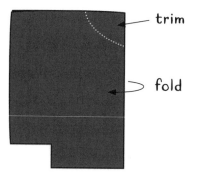

Open the jacket and lay it flat. Cut open the center front. Trim away the corners to make curved edges at the front neck and bottom edges of the jacket.

Use three strands of embroidery thread to sew blanket stitches up the side seams. Then stitch all around the outer edge. Sew on buttons and cut tiny slits for buttonholes.

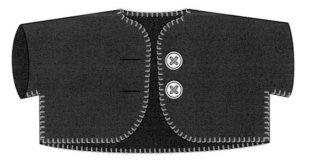

Cloche Hat

The cloche hat is bell shaped and hugs the head like a helmet. Invented in 1908, it became popular in the 1920s when short hairstyles for women became fashionable. You can add felt flowers, beads, buttons, or a feather to decorate it.

MATERIAL

Felt
Scissors
Needle and embroidery thread
Button

⦿ Use the pattern as a template. It's best to make one from scrap fabric first to be sure it will fit your doll. Adjust the pattern as needed. Cut two felt pieces for the hat, following cut line A for the front of the hat and cut line B for the back piece. Use embroidery thread and a blanket stitch to sew the pieces together along the seam line.

Use the patterns to make a felt flower with a leaf, or design your own. Cut the pieces from felt scraps and stitch them in place on the hat.

Sew a large button on for the flower center. You're done!

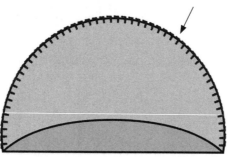

blanket stitch

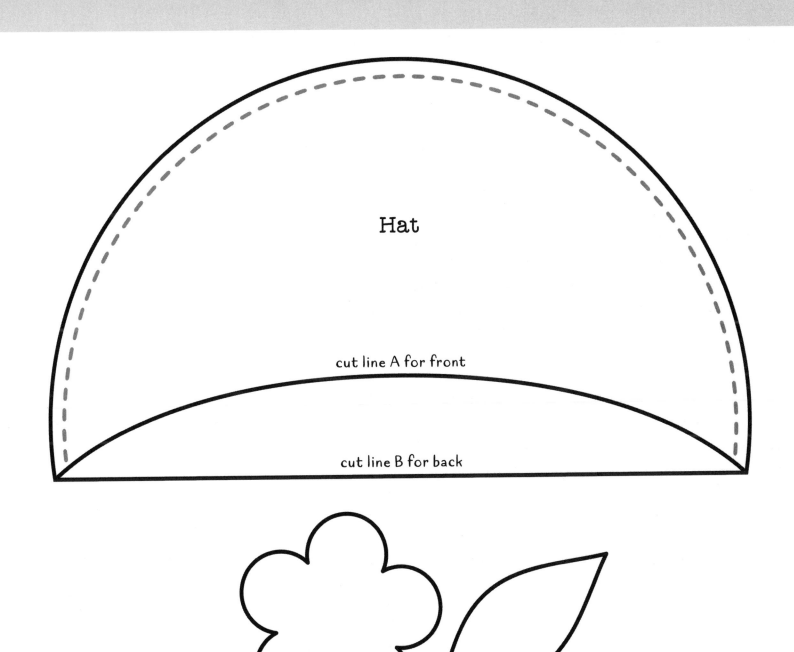

Hat

cut line A for front

cut line B for back

Sport Shoes

The pattern here will fit most 18-inch dolls, but you can adjust the pattern size to fit any doll. Make the shoes from craft foam and use permanent markers to add stripes or your own logo design. They can also be made of felt.

MATERIALS

Craft foam sheet (2 millimeters thick)
Pencil
Scissors
Needle and embroidery thread
2 lengths of thin yarn, each 14 inches long (for shoelaces)
Sewing pins

● If the patterns here fit your doll's foot, go ahead and use them. Trace the patterns onto foam with a pencil and cut out two shoe tops and two shoe soles.

If you need to create your own shoe pattern for your doll, stand the doll on the foam sheet and trace around its foot with a pencil. Hold the pencil straight up and down, so the tracing is accurate. Cut out the foam, which will be the shoe sole. Turn it over and trace around it to make another sole for the opposite foot. For the shoe top, use the pattern here but adjust it to fit your doll. Make a practice piece from scraps or paper to see what adjustments you need to make. Use your final pattern to cut out two shoe tops.

Join the two back seams of your shoe top on the outside, and secure them with a blanket stitch and matching thread. Match the dots on the sole to the back seam and to the center front of the shoe top. Don't use pins as they will leave holes in the foam. Just adjust the shoe as you sew so the pieces line up evenly. Sew all around, joining the shoe top to the sole with blanket stitch.

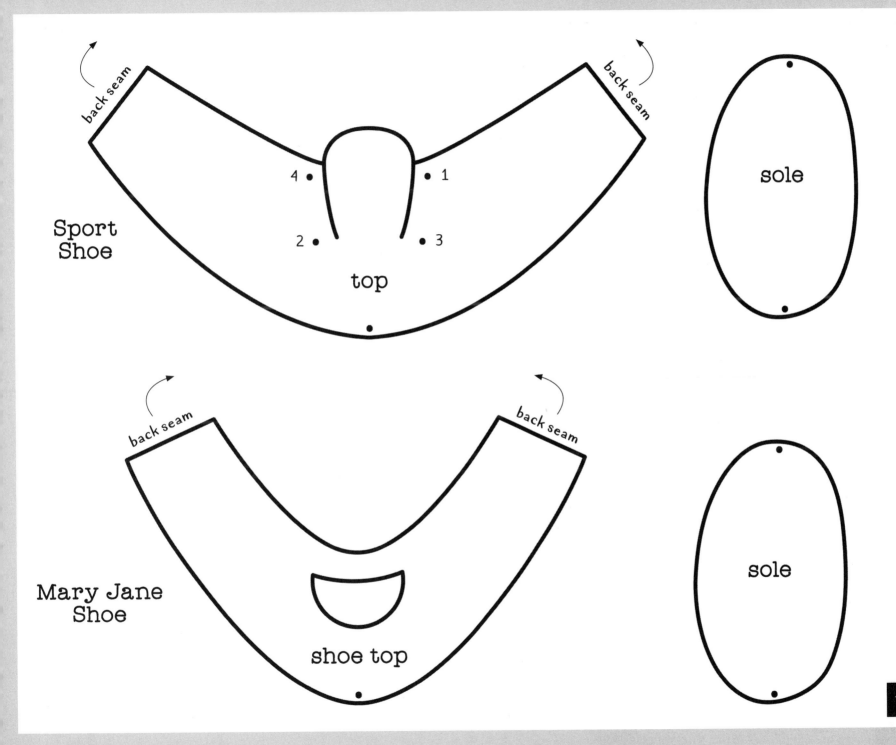

Sport Shoe

back seam

back seam

4 •   • 1

2 •   • 3

top

sole

Mary Jane Shoe

back seam

back seam

shoe top

sole

113

Thread an embroidery needle with about 14 inches of thin yarn. It will be a shoelace. Insert it through the shoe at #1 as shown on the pattern. Bring the needle back out at #2. Cross over and insert the needle at #3, and bring it out at #4. Pull the yarn gently to adjust the length so both laces are even.

Knot the ends of the yarn so they won't pull out of the shoe.

Repeat the process to create a second shoe, and you're done!

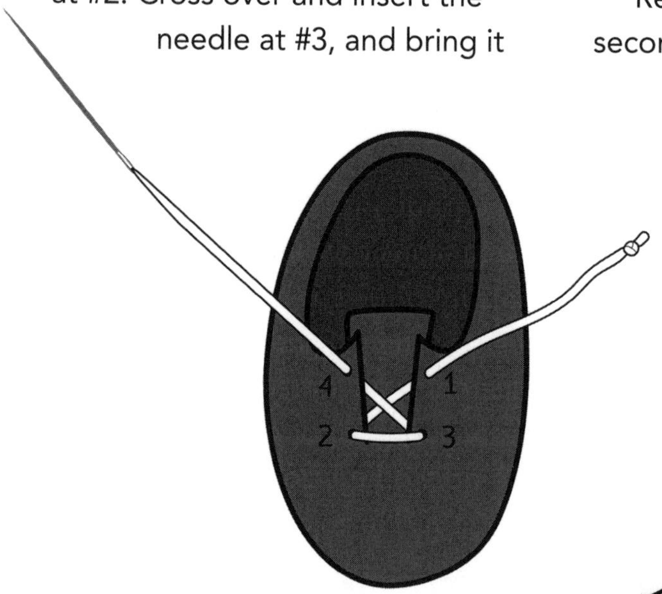

Mary Jane Shoes

Using foam craft sheets to make shoes is easy and fast. The shoes look like they are leather and can be made in lots of colors. Choose matching thread or try a contrasting color for variety. These Mary Janes look stylish with tops in bright red and soles in brown or black.

MATERIALS

Paper and pencil

Scissors

Foam craft sheet (2 millimeters thick)

Needle and sewing thread

Glue (optional)

Bead, button, or bow (optional)

⬤ Use the pattern on page 113 to create a paper pattern to fit your doll. Or you may need to trace your doll's foot, make a paper pattern, then a practice shoe.

Use the paper pattern to make two soles and two shoe tops from a foam sheet. Trace around the pattern with a pencil, then cut it out.

Join the two back seams of your shoe top on the outside, and stitch together using a blanket stitch and matching thread. Position the shoe top to fit the sole, matching up the dots on the sole with the back seam and front of the shoe. Stitch all around the outside edge with a blanket stitch. Glue on a bead or button to the strap if you want, or stitch a tiny bow in place on the shoe front.

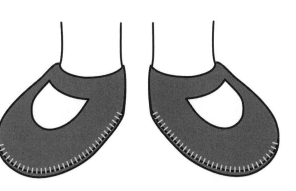

Handbag

Make this bag in any size you want. It can be a clutch (no strap) or cross-body bag with a long strap. It wouldn't hurt to have one to match every outfit.

MATERIALS

Pencil and paper
Felt
Scissors
Needle and embroidery thread
Button or large bead
Ribbon, cord, or long piece of felt

⦿ Use the patterns to cut a back and front from felt. Lay the front on the back, lining up the lower edges. Stitch the outside edges together along the front, leaving it open at the top, like a pocket. The top back will fold over the front of the bag.

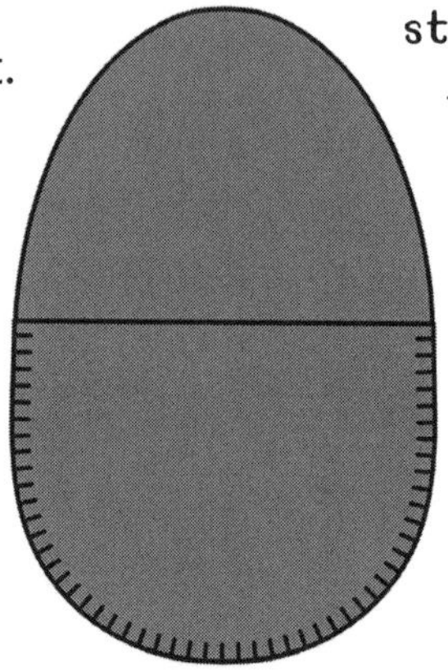

stitch front to back

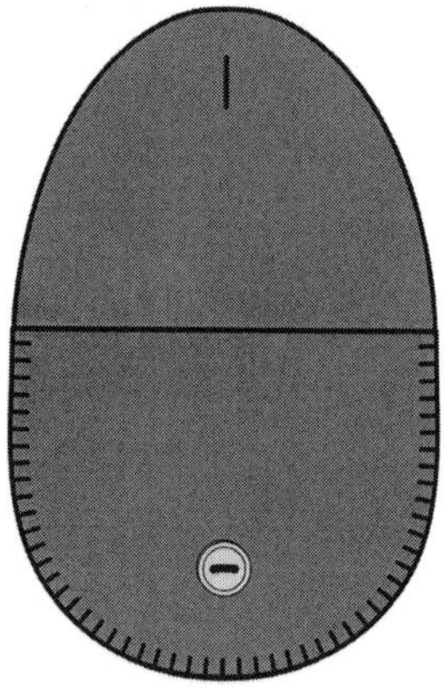

Sew a button or large bead to the front and cut a matching slit buttonhole in the top flap to fasten it.

Sew on a piece of ribbon or cord or cut a long strip felt for the strap. Stitch the ends in place under the flap, inside the bag, so they are hidden.

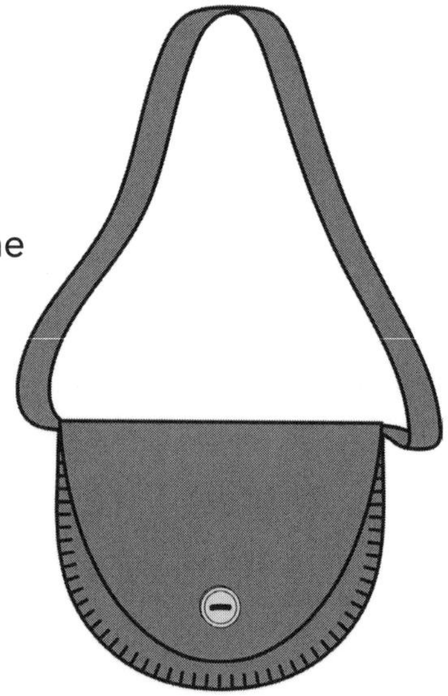

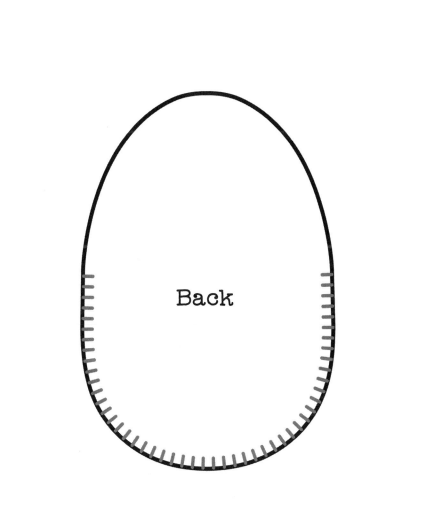

Back

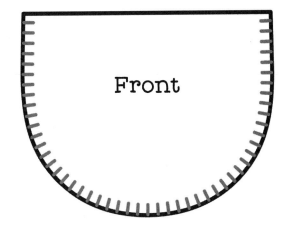

Front

Eyeglasses or Sunglasses

Lots of us wear glasses, so our dolls can, too. And sunglasses are for everybody, right? Well, now you can make several pairs for every doll—in colors to match their outfits. This design makes a pair that hinge at the corners so they can adjust to fit your doll without sliding off.

MATERIALS

Paper and pencil

Foam craft sheet (2 millimeters thick)

Scissors

2 small paper clips

Clear plastic packaging tape (2 inches wide)

Craft glue (optional)

Sequins, glitter, or other decorations (optional)

Permanent felt marker for sunglasses (black, blue, or brown color)

2 buttons (optional)

⬤ Trace the pattern below onto a foam sheet with a pencil and cut it out.

For each hinge, bend a paper clip open at the center and flatten it. Squeeze the sides together so it will hide behind the corners of the frame. Lay the frame flat on the table and position the flat paper clips at the corners. Apply a piece of clear tape onto the entire frame and lens openings, taping down the paper clips, too. Turn the tape-covered frame over and apply another piece of tape to the

other side of the frame and lens openings. Press the tape pieces together firmly, pressing out any wrinkles with your fingers.

Cut away the tape around the outer edge of the frame. Fold the paper clips at the corners to shape the glasses so they fit the doll's face. Add some glam to the frames: glue on sequins or squirt a band of glue along the frame and sprinkle glitter on it, then let dry.

For sunglasses, lay the glasses flat, with the inside facing up, and color the inside of the lenses with a permanent marker. Be sure it has dried and doesn't smudge off

bend paperclips open

before putting the sunglasses on your doll. You don't want stains on your doll's face.

If you are fitting a cloth doll with eyeglasses, you can sew two buttons in place on the sides of the head. The eyeglasses will rest on the buttons as if they were ears. They will be hidden by hair.

Tiny Teddy Bear

Of course your dolls need teddy bears! Make one (or two) for each of your dolls.

MATERIALS

Paper and pencil

Scissors

Felt: brown or tan for the body and pink or cream for the muzzle

Needle and embroidery thread (or glue)

Fine-tip permanent marker

Sewing pins

Stuffing

Chopstick or wooden skewer

Trace or copy the pattern pieces on page 121. Cut out two body pieces from brown felt and one muzzle from pink or cream felt.

Position the muzzle on the face and stitch (or glue) it in place. Draw the nose, mouth, and eyes with a permanent marker, or embroider them with black thread.

Pin the front and back together and stitch all around the outer edges using blanket stitches or short running stitches. Leave an opening to push stuffing into the body. Lightly stuff the bear, using a chopstick to push stuffing into the corners, then stitch the opening closed.

Body

Muzzle

Puppy

Puppy Dog

This puppy doesn't have four legs, so it's simple to make. *Tuck the puppy into your doll's handbag, backpack, or under its arm.*

MATERIALS

Paper and pencil
Scissors
Felt
Measuring tape or ruler
Needle and embroidery thread
Sewing pins
Stuffing
Wooden chopstick
Yarn or felt scrap (optional)

● Trace the pattern on page 121 with the paper and pencil. Use it to cut out two felt bodies.

Cut a strip of felt that measures 1 inch wide and 15 inches long. If you need to, sew two strips together to make a piece 15 inches long.

Using embroidery thread and working in a blanket stitch, sew one edge of the strip to one of the body pieces, stitching all around the body edge. Use sewing pins to secure the pieces while stitching. Line up the other body piece and pin it in place. Stitch the other body piece to the other side of the strip, leaving the area under the stomach open for stuffing.

Stuff the dog, pushing stuffing into the ears and legs with a chopstick if necessary. Sew the opening closed with blanket stitches. Use embroidery thread to stitch the eyes. Make a little dog collar from a piece of yarn or felt.

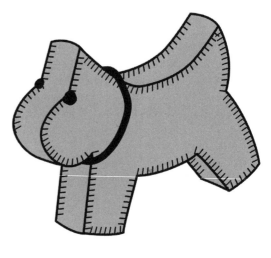

Mermaid Suit

W hat's a doll to do without a cute mermaid outfit? *Fin-ally you can make one for your doll. Your doll can even stand up in this outfit. This pattern fits an 18-inch doll but can be adjusted to fit other sizes.*

MATERIALS

Paper and pencil

Scissors

¼ yard knit fabric (or use an adult T-shirt)

Sewing pins

1 craft foam sheet (2 millimeters thick)

Needle and sewing thread to match the knit fabric

Felt square for the top, plus some scraps for flowers

1 sew-on snap set

Embroidery thread

Hair clip for doll (optional)

◉ Use the patterns on pages 67–68 for an 18-inch doll, or make your own pattern by laying your doll on paper and tracing from waist to ankles for the skirt of the suit. Be sure to hold the pencil straight up and down so you get an accurate measurement. Add ½ inch on both sides for seams. Since the knit fabric is a bit stretchy it will fit the doll smoothly.

Add a flippy fin to the bottom of the skirt pattern. Draw or tape it in place at the bottom of the suit. Cut out the pattern. Lay the T-shirt flat on the table, smoothing out wrinkles. Place the pattern on top, pin in place, and cut out two body pieces at once.

Go back to the paper pattern and cut the fin off the skirt at the ankle. Use that paper pattern to cut out one fin from the foam sheet. Trim about ¼ inch all around the fin edge so it will fit inside the suit.

Pin the two suit pieces together with the "wrong" side of the fabric, which was the inside of the

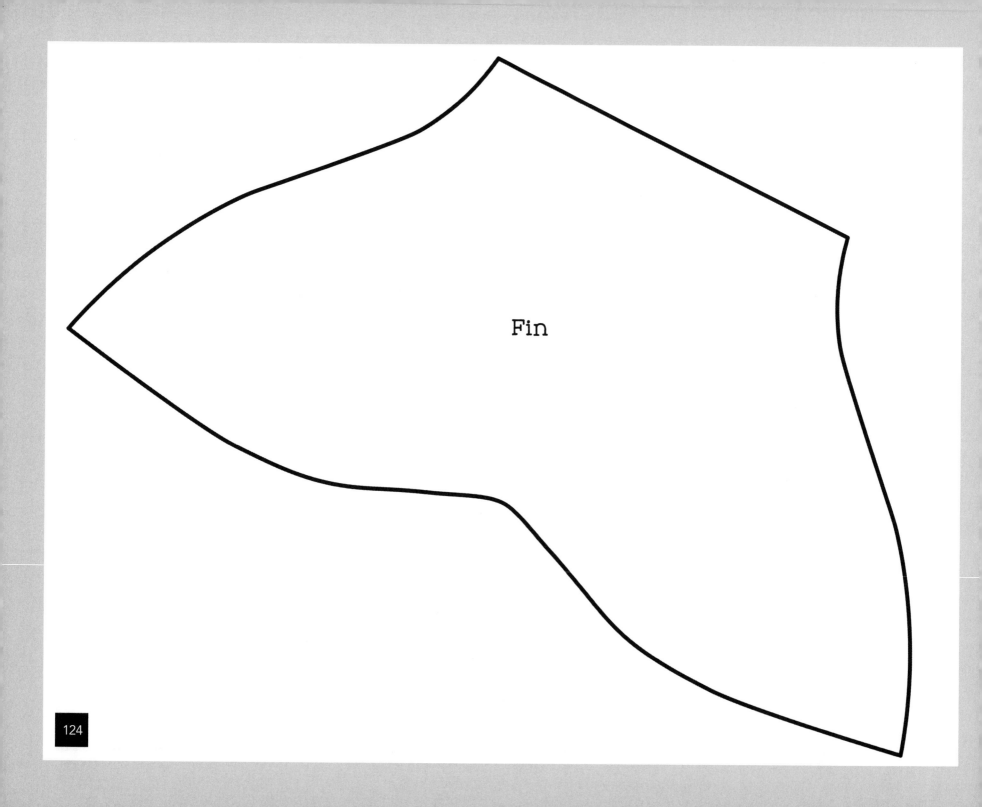

Fin

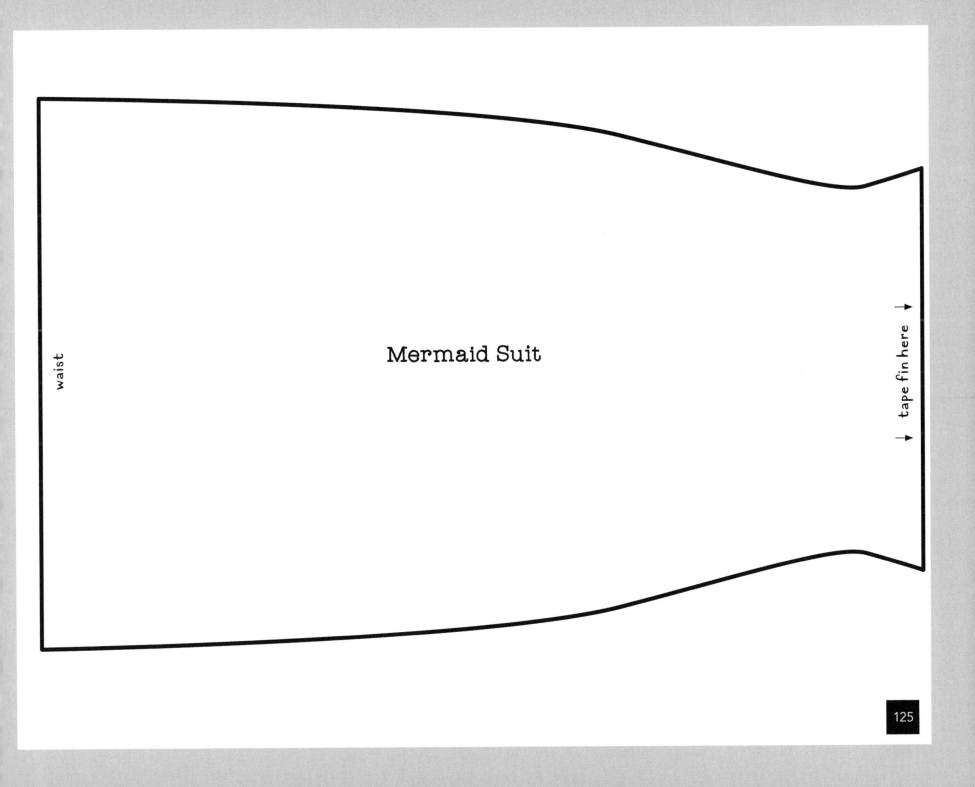

waist

Mermaid Suit

tape fin here

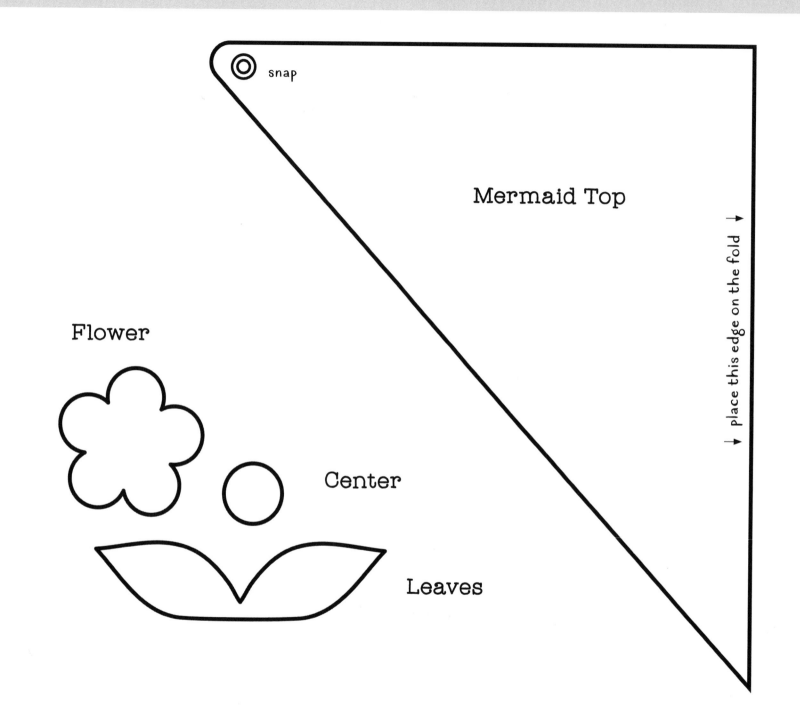

snap

Mermaid Top

place this edge on the fold

Flower

Center

Leaves

T-shirt, on the outside. After stitching, you'll turn it so the "right" side is on the outside with the seam hidden inside the suit.

With matching thread, stitch all around the outside seam of the suit, from one side waist to the other. Use a backstitch for best results, making small, even stitches. Use scissors to make clips in the seam fabric (but not through the stitching) at the curves of the ankle and fin. That way it will lie smooth when you turn it right side out. Fold under an inch at the waist and stitch it down so you have a waistband. Try it on the doll and stitch a few tucks at the waist if it is too loose.

Slip the foam fin piece into the bottom

clip seams at curves

clip seam

of the suit, fitting it inside the seam all around. It will help the fin maintain its shape.

Make the mermaid top from a felt square. If you're using an 18-inch doll, use the pattern on a folded square of felt. For other dolls, wrap the felt around the doll at its chest to figure out where to trim the fabric. Sew snaps on the back corners of the top. Use embroidery thread to make a blanket stitch on the top edge so the felt won't stretch out of shape.

Add some felt flowers: trace or draw the flower, center, and leaf shapes on felt and cut them out.

With a needle and thread, stitch through the center of the flower a few times to hold it all together, then stitch it in place on the top. Stitch or glue a matching flower to a hair clip for the doll's hair.

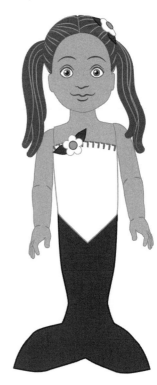

Doll Cake

Who wouldn't love a doll cake for a birthday or just for fun? It's easy to make a cake "skirt" to fit any size plastic doll. Decide what size skirt cake will fit your doll. You can even make smaller doll cakes using cupcakes!

ADULT SUPERVISION REQUIRED

MATERIALS

Plastic doll

Plastic food wrap

Pans or ovenproof bowls, greased and floured

2 cake mixes or 2 batches of the cake recipe below

2 cans of frosting, plus decorator icing and sprinkles

Cooling racks

Mixing bowl

Mixing spoon or electric mixer

Long-bladed bread knife

Large, flat plate or heavy cardboard

Spoons, knife, and spatula

⬤ You'll need a new plastic doll that will look good in a full-skirted gown. Remove the clothing and wrap the legs with plastic food wrap (so they will slide easily into the cake), and wind some wrap around the hair to keep it clean during the process.

Figure out how many skirt cakes you need depending on the doll's size and height. Assemble pans and measure if necessary. A 12-inch Barbie-size doll needs an 8-inch round pan, an 8-inch-wide oven-proof bowl, and a 5½-inch-wide ovenproof bowl. Other doll sizes may need different sizes of bowls, custard cups, and muffin pans. Tiny dolls can just slip into a cupcake.

You'll need two cake mixes or two batches of the cake recipe, and two cans of frosting. Use additional decorator icing and sprinkles, as desired. Prepare the pans by greasing and dusting with flour so the cakes come out of the pan easily. Get out the cooling racks, too, as the cakes need to sit on those after baking.

Prepare the mixes according to the package, or use this recipe, which is gluten-free and dairy-free so most everyone can enjoy it. You'll need to make two batches for most dolls.

Start by mixing together the following ingredients:

    4 eggs
    1¼ cup granulated cane sugar
    1 cup milk (dairy, coconut,
        or almond)
    2 teaspoons vanilla

Blend in the dry ingredients listed below, until the batter is smooth.

    1½ cups rice flour
    ¾ cup tapioca flour
    1 teaspoon salt
    1 teaspoon baking soda
    3 teaspoons baking powder
    1 teaspoon xanthan gum

When the batter is completely smooth, spoon into the prepared pans, filling each ⅔ full. Bake at 350 degrees for various times. The bowls may take an hour to bake because they are filled so deeply; the muffins or cupcakes may take about 20 minutes. Check often and test with a knife for doneness: insert a clean knife blade into the center of the cake and pull it out. If batter sticks to the blade, more baking time is needed. If it comes out clean, the cake is done.

Turn the cakes out of their pans and let cool on a rack.

Use a long-bladed bread knife to cut a small circle out of the center of each cake. It should be no wider than the doll's hips. Stack the cakes, lining up the centers, on a serving plate or circle of flat cardboard. As you stack them, put a layer of frosting on the top of each layer before placing the next cake onto it.

Brush off the crumbs and begin spreading frosting over the skirt.

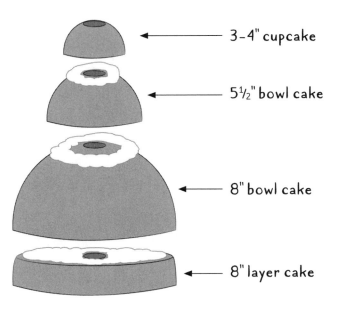

3–4" cupcake

5½" bowl cake

8" bowl cake

8" layer cake

Use a knife tip to draw pleats or designs. Add sprinkles or make swirls with a decorating tube.

Slip the doll down into the cake and cover its waist and chest with frosting: flowers, squiggles, or whatever designs you like. Pipe icing straps over the shoulders.

When you are done, sit back and enjoy. Be sure to take photos!

Dollhouses

Every doll needs a place to call home. Look around and gather materials to create a house and furniture for your favorite doll and her or his family. Below are some ideas for materials to get you started. These projects are more open-ended because the possibilities for doll homes are endless. Use your imagination and get creative! You can keep adding to, changing, and redecorating your houses for many years.

For Houses

- Large cardboard boxes or containers
- Lunch boxes
- Milk cartons
- Old suitcases

For Furniture

- Smaller boxes can be used to make beds, dressers, tables, chairs, and so on: shoe boxes, jewelry boxes, cell phone boxes, boxes used as packaging for toiletries or makeup, etc.

- Other packaging materials can be used for mattresses or cut up for pillows: foam, bubble wrap, jewelry box cotton lining, etc.

- Repurposed furniture from old playsets you no longer use

For Other Decor

- ⦿ Fabric scraps cut from old clothing, bedding, curtains, scarves, etc., for doll-sized bedding, pillows, rugs, and curtains
- ⦿ Gift wrap, calendar art, postcards, and pictures from magazines for wallpaper and wall art
- ⦿ Tin foil for mirrors
- ⦿ Plastic wrap for "water" in sinks or bathtubs

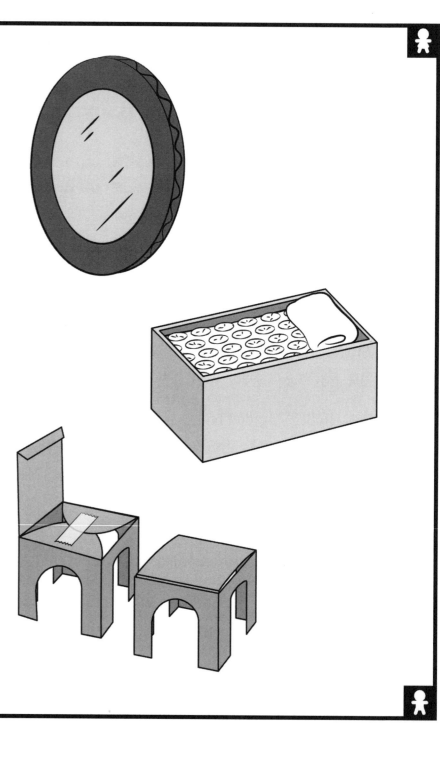

Lunch Box House

● Start small with a lunch box house. Old metal lunch boxes or vinyl-covered ones are perfect. You can use spray paint to cover the outside of the lunch box. Glue small printed paper, such as gift wrap or scrapbook paper, to the inside for wallpaper. Create a small bed from a cardboard box, with a homemade pillow and blanket. Add whatever else your doll needs. It can sleep inside the little house—just tuck it away in a quiet place.

Suitcase House

● For larger dolls, you can create a suitcase house, a step up from the lunch box house. Old hard plastic suitcases are perfect for this project. Spray paint the outside of the suitcase, and glue pieces of fabric to the inside for wallpaper or carpeting. Create several pieces of furniture from cardboard boxes and paper tubes. Store everything in the suitcase (even the doll) and slide it under your bed for safe keeping.

Simple Box House

● A box house can be as simple as one large cardboard box turned on its side. Cut out some windows, and draw decorations on the cardboard with markers or crayons. As you remodel the house, adding on more rooms, use duct tape to secure more boxes to the top and sides. Put together several boxes for a large condominium or apartment building for several dolls.

Four-Room House

⊙ Make a four-room fold-up house from large cartons or lightweight cardboard. With an adult's help, use a serrated bread knife to saw sections from large grocery or moving boxes. Cut two rectangles, then cut slits in the center halfway through each rectangle. Draw or paint windows and wallpaper. Glue on foil for mirrors. Cut a door that opens to the next room.

Slip the two sections together by sliding the two slits together. Now you have four rooms, which can be filled with folded paper furniture and small cardboard box decor. Add some felt or cloth rugs. You can make tiny houses like this from two index cards if you want, for little bendy dolls.

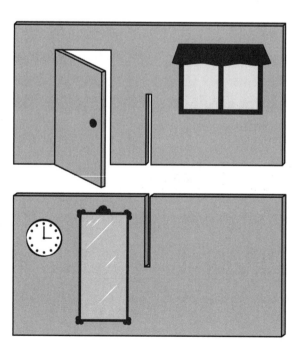

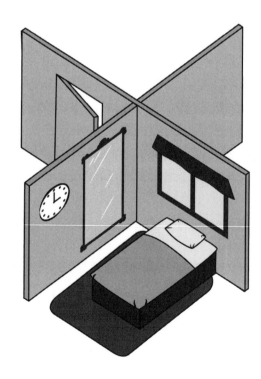

Fold-Up House

Most of us don't have enough space for a large dollhouse, so here's how to make one for an 18-inch doll that folds flat when you aren't playing with it.

ADULT SUPERVISION REQUIRED

MATERIALS

Ruler or measuring tape
Pencil
Cardboard (corrugated)
Heavy-duty scissors or craft knife
Duct tape

● Ask an adult to help you cut five squares, each measuring 20 by 20 inches. Cut two rectangles, 10 by 20 inches each.

Wrap duct tape around the edges of each piece so the pieces are strong and have a clean finish.

Tape the two rectangles together to make a square. That will be the fold-up floor. Assemble and tape together the two sides and the two roof pieces. Tape the back to one side.

Now you can set the house up. Fold all the pieces up and together so the two floor pieces sit at the bottom and the two roof pieces join at the top. Hold the back in place with some tape.

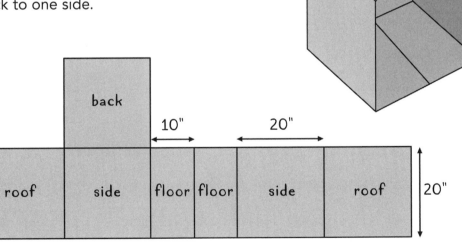

back

10"

20"

roof | side | floor | floor | side | roof

20"

When you are through playing, unfasten the tape at the back so the cardboard folds on one side. Push up the center of the floor and the house will collapse and fold flat.

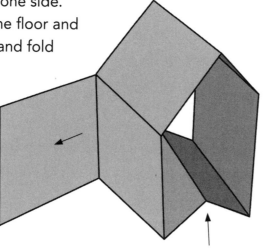

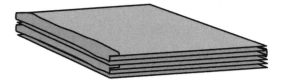

Doll Museum

There are hundreds of doll museums around the country and the world. If you get a chance, visit them. Some museums include toys, too, and often dollhouses and furniture. They are usually created from someone's collection of dolls that got too large for his or her home or was passed on to a museum after the collector's death. In some museum collections, you will see many types of dolls in a variety of clothing styles. If the exhibit has very old dolls, you can see how they were made in the past. Other museums concentrate on only one type of doll, such as Barbie. Doll museums, like other museum collections, depend on what the collector was interested in.

If you enjoy making dolls, you will soon have a room crowded with your collection. Create your own museum to show them off while letting others learn more about dolls and doll making.

MATERIALS

Your favorite dolls and doll accessories
Doll stands or little doll chairs
Index cards, 3 by 5 inches
Marker or pen
Tape (optional)

● Think about a goal for your doll museum. Just a haphazard group of various dolls is not interesting to the viewer, and it can be confusing. Maybe your museum will focus on one type of doll, such as sock dolls or folk dolls or paper dolls. If you want to collect and repaint plastic dolls, that could be interesting to others, too. Take before-and-after photos to show what the dolls looked like before you made the changes, and post them next to the dolls as part of the exhibit. Maybe you want to show dolls as art forms and educate others how to make them, too.

Gather the dolls and doll stands or little chairs for them to perch on. Use an index card for each doll to make a plaque or caption like you see in many museums.

Write a description of the doll—its name, the date it was made, what materials it's made of—any and all interesting facts you know about the doll. Post each card next to its corresponding doll by either taping it up nearby or folding the bottom edge of the card back to form a stand.

Your doll museum can start small, with maybe a shelf or two of a bookcase where you display dolls so friends and family can view them. The next step might be to outfit an old suitcase as a minimuseum. Moving from a suitcase exhibit, you can think about larger spaces, such as a room, garden shed, corner of a shop or classroom, or even a traveling van or trailer. Museums can even be totally online—create a website to share your dolls with the world.

After you put your museum together, be sure to keep it clean and organized. You may want to use a small notebook as a guest book, where visitors can sign their names and write comments.

Whatever you do, enjoy learning and sharing. And keep making dolls!